Be Strong, My Abela

Berlie Doherty

Be Strong, My Abela

Annotations by
Mechthild Hesse

Ernst Klett Sprachen
Stuttgart

1. Auflage 1 5 4 3 2 1 | 2014 13 12 11 10

Internetadresse: www.klett.de / www.lektueren.com

Abridged by: Alan Brown
Redaktion: Paul Newcomb
Layoutkonzeption: Elmar Feuerbach
Gestaltung und Satz: Satzkasten, Stuttgart
Umschlaggestaltung: Elmar Feuerbach
Titelbild: shutterstock (Charlene Bayerle), New York, NY
Druck und Bindung: AZ Druck und Datentechnik GmbH, Heisinger Straße 16, 87437 Kempten/Allgäu
Printed in Germany

ISBN 978-3-12-578025-5

Contents

Berlie Doherty
(reproduced by permission of Andersen Press, London)

About the author

Berlie Doherty was born near Liverpool and is best known for her books for young adults. She has won the Carnegie Medal twice, for *Dear Nobody* and then for *Granny is a Buffer Girl.* Her other works include novels for adults, plays for theatre and radio, television series and libretti for children's opera. There are also dramatised versions of *Dear Nobody* and *The Snakestone,* two of her stories for young adults.

Doherty went to Upton Hall Convent School in Liverpool. She studied English at the University of Durham, and then social science at the University of Liverpool. Following this, she did a teaching course in Sheffield. During this time, she wrote her first short story. Her first book was published in the early 80s and she became a full-time writer soon afterwards.

Doherty is inspired by landscape, and she lives in a beautiful part of Britain, in Edale, Derbyshire: many of her books are set in this part of Britain, called the Peak District.

Doherty often works with children and teenagers when developing her novels, having "a conviction that children are the experts and I can always learn from them." She read her first novel, *How Green You Are!* to one of her classes while working as a teacher in Sheffield. *Tough Luck* (1987) was written while she was working as a writer at a school, while her research for *Spellhorn* included extensive work with a group of blind children in Sheffield.

Other works for young adults include *Dear Nobody,* which has also been published in an annotated version by Klett, *Daughter of the Sea, Street Child* and *The Snakestone.*

About the book

Be Strong, My Abela is a shortened version of the very successful *Abela: The Girl Who Saw Lions*. It is the story of two girls. One lives in Tanzania, the orphaned child of a family that has to live with the horror of HIV/Aids. When her uncle sends her to England, her grandmother thinks she is going to a better life; but he is involved in crime and Abela's future does not look good. Her mother's dying words to her had been: "Be strong, my Abela, be strong," and these words give her the strength and courage to survive.

The other girl is Rosa, who lives in Sheffield, UK, with her mother. They do everything together, including learning to skate at IceSheffield. Rosa doesn't really want anything in her life to change, until one day her mother tells her she is thinking of adopting another child. Rosa is very upset. "What if I had said to her, 'I'm thinking of adopting another mother?'"

Berlie Doherty's inspiration for *Abela* came when she visited Tanzania, which she found very beautiful — its people, animals, and the landscape. She was encouraged by two workers there to write about HIV/Aids in Africa. She had also been interested in the subject of adoption for many years, having been a social worker at the beginning of her working life.

So that young adults learning English can gain maximum enjoyment from this beautiful story, this edition has been especially abridged and slightly simplified from the original by accomplished author in his own right, Alan Brown.

Chapter 1

ABELA

The priest arrived on a red motorbike. Dust rose like smoke around him as he roared into the village. Already the villagers were strolling towards the church, which was built like a barn on wooden supports. The sides were open, and swallows and children swooped and tumbled in and out. Abela was one of the first to arrive, carrying her baby sister on her hip, the child's skinny arms looped round her neck. She was too big to be carried really, and Abela was too small to be carrying her. When she found her seat she lowered her sister on to the sandy ground and shook her shoulders to ease them. Nyota could walk now, but wouldn't. She sat gazing listlessly up at Abela, sometimes whimpering to herself, sometimes completely silent. The music and singing might distract her for a while, or might send her off to sleep. She was poorly, Abela knew that. There were many poorly babies in the village. Her grandmother, Bibi, told her there was no hope for any of them.

One of Abela's neighbours squeezed along the row to sit next to her. "Where's your Mama?" she asked. She had to shout over the noise of chattering and bird cries in the church.

"Mama's tired." Abela said.

"She poorly too?" The neighbour clicked her tongue and shifted herself round in her creaking seat.

Abela turned her head away and watched the priest. She had nothing to say. Mama was sick. The baby was dying. Baba was dead. What was there to say?

2 **Abela** [ə'belə] – 5 **to stroll** [strəʊl] to walk in a relaxed way – 5 **barn** large farm building – 6 **support** [sə'pɔ:t] *here: Untergrund* – 6 **swallow** *Schwalbe* – 7 **to swoop and tumble** to move downwards suddenly and fast – 12 **Nyota** [naɪ'jəʊtə] – 13 **to gaze** to look – 13 **listless** not paying attention because you are tired or ill – 14 **to whimper** to make low crying sounds – 16 **poorly** *(inf)* ill – 19 **to squeeze** to try to get into a small space – 21 **to chatter** to talk continuously about unimportant things

The priest was unlocking the pannier of his motorbike. He brought out a green carrier bag and took out his altar vestments, his long white robe, his gorgeous red embroidered chasuble and stole. He slipped them over his jeans and tee shirt and tucked his white collar into place. Then he walked into church carrying a tin of dried milk powder, which he placed on the altar table. He turned to face the congregation, and lifted his arms wide so his robes unfolded like wings around him. The chattering stopped. He began to sing, and immediately everyone joined in, fitting harmonies round his deep rich voice. The hymn was like a river flowing with currents of different colours. Abela always thought the sound she made when she was singing was yellow, golden-yellow like corn. Mama's was a pretty shivering blue. And Baba's – Baba's used to be brown. But Baba's voice would never be heard again.

"Please, please don't let Mama die too. Don't let Nyota die. Don't. Don't."

On the day Baba died, Mama had shaved her head to show she was in mourning for her husband. She sat outside their mud hut and all their belongings were brought out – their bedrolls, the cooking pots, the blankets and baskets. Her husband's younger brother moved into the hut, because he was nearly a man now, too old to be sharing a hut with his parents and his sisters.

At last Mama's mother, Bibi, had come to fetch them to her own house in the next village.

"One day soon," Bibi had said, "the hyena will come for me, and this will be your home. And the field that goes with it," she added, gazing out at the little strip of land that was their

1 **pannier** [ˈpæniə] small bag or basket for a bike or motorbike – 3 **vestments** *(fml)* clothes – 3 **gorgeous** [gɔ:dʒəs] very beautiful – 3 **to embroider** *sticken* – 4 **chasuble** [ˈtʃæzʊbəl] **and stole** *Messegewand und Stola* – 9 **immediately** [ɪˈmi:diətli] *sofort* – 11 **hymn** [hɪm] song which is sung in church *(Hymne)* – 11 **current** *Stromschnelle* – 14 **to shiver** to shake *(zittern)* – 19 **in mourning** when a person dies you are in mourning – 20 **mud** wet earth *(Lehm)* – 21 **bedroll** bed that rolls up; mattress – 27 **hyena** [haɪˈi:nə] wild animal similar to a dog

family's only wealth. "Your brother won't want it, now he's in England Europe."

The priest used the key of his motorbike to prise open the lid of the dried milk tin, and brought out of it the discs of unleavened wafer bread. By the mystery of his prayers the bread would become the body of Christ. Abela knew that was so, even though it still looked like bread, and was so fine and light that it melted on her tongue and clung to the roof of her mouth.

"Lamb of God," the priest said, "Who takest away the sins of the world..."

The rainbow river of song poured through the church again, and the rich loud sound of it filled Abela with hope. God would hear it and make Mama well. Her golden voice shimmered all the way to heaven. Of course Mama wouldn't die.

We have a game, Mama and I, when we pound maize. When the corncobs have been drying in the sun for long enough, we shake off all the little yellow buds into a heap, and we pour them into a basket. They go tchick, tchick, as they trickle down. Then we grind the buds into flour. We pound it with the end of a long stick from a tree, which is just as tall as Mama. It takes so long that our legs ache and ache with standing and our arms are heavy with holding the branch and stamping it down again and again. We must do it for hours, every day when the corn is ripe, to make enough for our food, to make enough to sell. The sky is greasy and sweaty. Flies buzz round my face and walk on my skin, and because my hands are busy I can't brush them away. They crawl in my hair and I can't do anything about them. My head throbs and I'm thirsty and tired.

1 **wealth** [welθ] large amount of money and property *(Reichtum)* – 3 **to prise open** to open sth with difficulty – 4 **unleavened** [ʌn'levənd] **wafer bread** *Hostien ohne Hefe gebacken* – 8 **to cling** to stick – 8 **roof** *here:* top – 9 **lamb** [læm] *Lamm* – 9 **sin** something that is very wrong *(Sünde)* – 11 **to pour** [pɔ:] **through** to spread *(here: sich ergießen)* – 15 **to pound** [paʊnd] to beat or hit very hard – 16 **corncob** *Maiskolben* – 17 **bud** *Knospe* – 18 **to trickle** *rinnen* – 19 **to grind** [graɪnd] *mahlen* – 21 **to ache** [eɪk] to cause pain *(schmerzen)* – 25 **greasy** [gri:si] full of fat – 28 **to throb** *klopfen, pochen*

This is when the game starts. Just when I think I can't do any more, Mama shouts, "One, Abela!" She raises her branch and then she let go of it and she claps her hands before she catches it again. I do the same. It's hard to keep the pounding rhythm going. *Pound lift drop clap catch pound lift drop catch.* Mama sings while we're doing it. When we've got a nice smooth rhythm going she shouts "Two, Abela!" She lets go of her branch and claps twice before she catches it again. *Pound lift drop clap-clap catch pound lift drop clap-clap* … My face is twisted with concentration and my hands are so sweaty that the branch slides through them. Mama is singing and my chest is tight with wanting to laugh. The rhythm flows, smooth as a dance, and then Mama shouts "Three, Abela!" But it's impossible. We bend over with laughter, it hiccups out of me like the little yellow buds of corn, and Mama's laughter peals out like pretty bells, blue and shivery and sweet. And when we look down, the flour is made.

But we don't play that game now. Mama doesn't stand with me while I'm pounding corn. She lies in the cool darkness of Bibi's hut, and she doesn't laugh any more.

I am not afraid of anything. I am not afraid of the mad mzee who comes down to the market sometime. She is not like my grandmother mzee, Bibi. She is like a wounded animal. We don't have a proper stall in the market, under the shade of the thatch, because we are too poor. We spread a cotton kanga on the ground and sit on it, and Mama and I make little heaps of the things we have brought to sell; red beans sometimes, or yellow cobs of corn, or oranges that a neighbour has swopped with us. If we have been given green bananas we lay them out

7 **smooth** [smu:ð] *opp of:* rough – 10 **to twist** to turn around quickly and suddenly – 11 **to slide** to move slowly and smoothly – 12 **tight** *opp of:* loose – 15 **bud** *Knospe* – 15 **to peal** to make a loud sound – 17 **flour** [flaʊə] main ingredient of bread and cake *(Mehl)* – 21 **mzee** Swahili word for older person – 23 **wounded** ['wu:ndɪd] – 24 **stall** stand – 25 **thatch** straw – 25 **kanga** Swahili word for rectangular piece of cloth which is wrapped around the body – 28 **to swop** to give something and to get something in return

in a bunch, like the fingers of a hand. If we sell enough to buy some other food from someone else, we are happy.

But then the mad mzee comes hobbling round the stalls with her panga tucked under her arm. This panga is a very sharp curved blade that is used for cutting down the corn. My father once told me that he had seen a man slice another man's head clean off his neck with a panga, because he had tried to steal his cow. And the mad mzee comes with her panga, muttering and grumbling and staring at people, and if she thinks you are a stranger or you are laughing at her, or she doesn't like your face that day, she waves her panga in the air and lurches towards you. I'm not afraid when she chooses me, because I can run, and she can only stamp her feet on the ground and stumble forward a few paces. I can run to the chilli-seller's stall and hide under it, and when the mad mzee finds me she bends down shrieking and wallering, and I see the blade like a silver tongue sipping the air for me. I can back away and shimmy under the next stall.

In the end she forgets me and chases another child or the white lady teacher Mrs Long, until somebody holds out a cigarette to her. This is what she wants. She tucks the cigarette behind her ear and shuffles away home, and the gossiping in the market starts again, and somebody puts on the tape of Mister Bing Crosby singing '*I'm dreaming of a white Christmas*,' which we all love so much. No, I'm not afraid of the mad mzee.

And I'm not afraid of the lion. Simba. The lions live up in the purple mountains and they never come down to the village in the daytime. At night we sometimes hear the maize crinkling as they step through it, and we lie in the darkness with our breath as soft as moths, and my Mama's hand creeps out to me and closes over mine. But Simba won't come into our hut, and

11 **to lurch** to walk or move suddenly – 14 **to stumble forward a few paces** *ein paar Schritte vorwärts stolpern* – 16 **to waller** ['wɒle] *(inf)* to shout – 16 **blade** sharp side/edge of a knife *(Klinge)* – 19 **to chase** to follow sb quickly in order to catch that person – 22 **to shuffle** to walk slowly making soft noises with your feet – 22 **to gossip** to speak about other people behind their back – 30 **moth** small flying insect *(Motte)*

we won't go out in the darkness of the night, so I'm not afraid of him.

I am not afraid of the little monkeys who drop down on me from the trees and squeal and jabber down my ear and pull my hair with their tight little fists. They snatch food from my hands and gobble it up. I hate them sometimes, but I'm not afraid of them.

I have never been afraid of anything till now. Now I'm afraid that my Mama is going to die.

Chapter 2

ROSA

Far, far away from Africa, in a northern England city called Sheffield, it was beginning to snow. It came in such a short, sharp flurry that it was over before a lot of people knew it had started, but when they looked out of the window or left their offices and schools to catch the bus home, they found a white layer covering everything, softening all the sharp angles of the buildings, making the pavements slithery.

Mum was standing in the kitchen, leafing through the *Big Issue* that she had bought in town. She opened it at a particular page and smoothed the spine down to keep it open there. She laid it flat on the table. Rosa glanced at it. It showed a picture of black children in a dusty compound. *A Desperate Situation*, the headline read. Twitchy jumped on top of the magazine and mewed plaintively to remind her it was food time.

"I got two birthday cards," Rosa said. "And twenty pounds, Mum! *Twenty*!"

"Nana and Grandpa will be bringing something," Mum said. "They'll be here soon. I hope this snow doesn't hold them up."

Rosa ran upstairs. She opened her wardrobe door and clicked the clothes hangers along the rail one by one – blue dress, no, yellow skirt, no, brown skirt, no, green cords, no, blue jeans! She pulled out her new jeans with the flowery patch pockets and a red polo-necked sweater, wriggled out of her school uniform, and she was dressed and down the stairs before Nana and Grandpa came through the door. Grandpa lifted her off the ground and squeezed her against him like a cushion. His clothes and his beard were wet with sprinkles of snow.

9 **slithery** slippery – 11 ***Big Issue*** magazine in the UK sold by homeless people on the street. The "issues" *(politische Fragen)* in the magazine are about homeless people. – 14 **compound** an enclosed area – 14 **desperate** very bad – 16 **mewed** [mjʊ:d] **plaintively** the cat made a high, sad sound

"I can only just do that now!" he laughed. "You're nearly a giant. Anyone would think you were thirteen years old."

"I am! I am!" Rosa shouted, leaning back and pretending to batter him with her fists. "Put me down, you monster!"

"Calm down," Nana said. "You're a young lady now, Rosa." She opened up her carrier bag and brought out a present wrapped, as always, in Christmas paper. Nana never saw the point of buying special birthday paper, at any time of the year. Rosa looked at her Mum excitedly. Was it, could it be, the present she had dreamed of? She tore open the paper, opened the box, and screamed with joy. It was. It was a pair of ice skates.

I love skating, more than anything else in the world. Mum and I are learning together. We go to the skating rink every Saturday morning, and we are in the same class. We're just about as good as each other. I can go backwards, I can go in circles, I can criss-cross. I love the music, which makes me want to dance and sing, and the sounds of the skates *freeshing* on the ice. I love the excitement I feel when I try a new move, and try and try again because it's too hard at first, and then find out I can do it. Most of all, I love it because it's something my mum and I do together.

So we started having lessons, and to our surprise Mum turned out to be quite good at it, and so did I. We wouldn't miss our Saturday skating lesson for anything. Since we started ice-skating we've got into the habit of having to do particular things each time we go, a set of traditions like a sort of good luck charm. The first is that we always travel to Ice Sheffield on the supertram. The tram is perfect, because it glides so smoothly and quietly you could believe it was on skates and saying, "Look at me! I can do it too!"

3 **to pretend** to do as if – 6 **carrier bag** [ˈkæriə] shopping bag – 7 **Nana** grandma – 26 **to get into the habit** to start doing sth regularly – 26 **particular** [pəˈtɪkjələ] certain, specific – 27 **good luck charm** *Glücksbringer*

When we arrive at the Arena stop I race Mum up the track to Ice Sheffield – I always beat her and have to wait at the door. Then she has to wait for me while I get my hire boots. She has her own boots because her feet have stopped growing. Just before we step on the ice, she squeezes my hand.

"Don't .." she says.

"Break .." I say.

"Anything!" we both say, and then we're off, skating as fast as we can round the rink, and we lose each other because we're in a tide of people, all swaying and gliding, drifting, dancing. It's like the river swim at Pond's Forge; you just have to go with the current, leaning into the bends like a cyclist, round and round, swift and sure, a swarm of coloured fish.

Our coaches call us into our groups and the next forty minutes are really hard work, going backwards and forwards across the rink, swirling, making lemon shapes with our feet, scissoring, turning, weaving, going down on one knee and gliding up again. It's really difficult. I don't have time to look at anyone then, I just so much want to get it right. I'm only aware of one thing, and that's my ice shadow. She goes everywhere with me, turns with me, glides under my skates and comes round the other side. I know I shouldn't watch her because my eyes are supposed to be looking straight ahead, but it's like having a sister, a twin, my black self with me all the time.

When the coaching finishes the music comes on, and we're all grace and speed, all swans now, every one of us, floating free as air because we don't have to concentrate any more. Then Mum's next to me, holding out her hand, and we glide round together. We both gasp and laugh out loud with the fun of it. Everything seems to fall away from us; all the skaters and the watchers and the coaches, it's just me and Mum, holding hands and looking at each other and laughing, ready to fly.

3 **hire boots** boots that you pay money for so that you can borrow them for a short period of time – 10 **tide of people** crowd – 11 **Forge** [fɔ:dʒ] *Schmiede* – 26 **grace** a smooth way of moving

The thing about Mum is, - I can't say this to her, I can't really say this to anybody, because it sounds a bit silly, - but, well, I think she's my best friend. And that's why the skating, learning together and having fun together and holding hands and swinging each other round – that's why it's my favourite thing.

"We've passed to level nine today," Mum told me one day, just before my birthday. "We've got to decide what to do when we finish that. Figure skating or ice hockey."

"Do we have to choose?" I asked her.

"If we still want coaching, we do."

"Figure skating."

"That's fine." Mum poured herself another coffee. "I'm thinking of doing ice hockey."

I stared at her. I couldn't believe it. This is what *we* do together; this is our special thing.

She screwed the lid back on her flask. "Back to the ice? Fifteen more minutes, then we'll have to catch the tram."

And not long after that, Mum told me about the adoption child.

We were on the supertram, on the way to Ice Sheffield for a public session. She moved across from the seat facing me so she was sitting next to me, and said,

"Rosa, I've got something very special to ask you. How would you like to have a sister?"

I nearly burst with surprise and excitement. "Mum! Really? Oh, cool! Are you going to have a baby?"

She shook her head, smiling. "You're pleased, aren't you? But no, I'm not having a baby. I'm thinking of adopting a little girl."

That was how she broke it to me.

"What do you think? What do you think, Rosa?"

What was I supposed to think? I said nothing, nothing at all. How could I say anything, there on the tram, or anywhere,

8 **figure skating** *Eiskunstlaufen* – 16 **to screw a lid on a flask** to close the bottle (flask = *Thermosflasche*) – 25 **to burst with surprise** [sə'praɪz] to be very surprised – 29 **to break sth to sb** to tell sb exciting or important news

how could I tell her how I felt? I didn't want an adopted sister. I didn't really want another child in our house at all. A baby was one thing; I could play with it and take it out in the pram. It might even look like me. But an adopted sister? What if I had said to her, "I'm thinking of adopting a mother?" How would she have felt? Inside my head I was screaming. If I opened my mouth, all that would have come out would have been a scream.

I turned my face away from her and stared at my reflection in the window. Mum couldn't talk now, there were some kids opposite us talking and laughing noisily. She tried to hold my hand instead. I balled it up into a fist. She stroked the fist. She lifted my balled fist up and kissed it, and in my reflection I saw my eyes glisten with tears.

3 **pram** baby carriage, buggy – 14 **to glisten** ['glɪsən] **with tears** to start to cry

Chapter 3

ABELA

During the night my grandmother Bibi woke me up, shaking my shoulder, hissing in my ear, "Abela, Abela, get up now."

It was pitch dark. My eyes were sticky with sleep. I rolled away from her and she shook me again, "Abela, your Mama's very sick."

When there is no light there is no body, only a hissing voice and a hard hand gripping your shoulder. It brings fear; it brings such hopelessness, when there is no light anywhere. I fumbled across the floor to where my mother lay. She was so hot that I could feel her skin burning before I touched her. Hot, and wet, and her breath dry like wind rattling leaves.

"Mama, what's wrong?" I whimpered.

"It's time to take her to the hospital," Bibi said.

"Now?"

"Yes, yes, the sooner the better. I can't do anything more for her."

I was still stupid with sleep, shaking with tiredness and fright. The hospital was in the town, more than a day's walk away for a fit man. I didn't understand what my grandmother wanted me to do.

"You must go with her, now," she insisted. "I'll stay with Nyota."

Numb, I wrapped my kanga round myself, and my grandmother put a blanket round my shoulders. Last year my mother and I had walked my father to the hospital, one each side of him, and he leaned on her the whole time. We trudged

5 **pitch dark** very dark – 10 **to fumble across** *sich vortasten* – 20 **fright** fear – 23 **to insist** to say sth over and over again in order to convince sb to do sth – 25 **numb** [nʌm] without feeling anything – 28 **to trudge** [trʌdʒ] to walk with slow heavy feet

and swayed and stopped, trudged and swayed and stopped. The sun had come and gone twice before we had arrived.

"How can I do it on my own?" I whispered. "You must come too."

"I can't," my grandmother said. "I must look after Nyota." She had my sister in her arms, wrapped tightly in her kanga. I felt for her cold little baby hand, and knew then that I would never see my sister again.

"Bring her too," I urged.

"And we'd walk as slow as elephants. No, take your mother, and go as quickly as you can. Maybe the doctors can save her. I can't."

My mother groaned and sat up on the edge of her bed, and between us Bibi and I lifted her to her feet.

"Can you walk, Mama?" I whispered.

"Yes, I can walk."

My grandmother put into our hands the branches we used for pounding the corn. "These will help you," she said, "And you will be able to protect yourselves with them, too."

I remembered once when I was very little, my Baba gave me a long stick that would fight off lions. "Look big and stern," he used to say, "And wave your stick at them. Shout your head off! Then see how Simba runs away." And he would laugh his honey laugh at the way I drew myself up to my full height and brandished my stick and roared at the pretend lions. It was a game, that day.

So we set out, with the blanket spread across Mama's shoulders and mine, even though my mother protested that she was hot. I could feel her skin raging like fire. The earth was cool under our feet. We could see that the sky was nearly white with stars that were as bright as fireflies. Nobody moved in the village, everybody slept, but as soon as we left the cluster of huts I knew that the beasts of the night were

1 **to sway** to move from one side to the other, all the time as though you are about to fall over – 9 **to urge** [ɜːdʒ] to say strongly, to insist – 13 **to groan** to moan *(stöhnen)* – 21 **stern** serious – 25 **to brandish** to wave sth like a weapon around in a threatening way – 33 **cluster of huts** small group of huts built together near to each other

prowling, watching and waiting, stalking hungrily. Sometimes a sharp scream splintered the silence, and we knew that some creature had been taken. And the more I listened, the more I heard, creaking and scratching, padding and slithering; a quick yapping here, a flurry of wingbeats there.

Mama leaned heavily on her stick, but after a bit she put her free arm across my shoulders, and I put my arm around her waist.

Sometimes she hummed a little tune, and sometimes I sang the lovely songs we learnt at school and at church. We were both glad when the light came at last, but the sky was a greasy grey and the air was clammy. It grew hotter and hotter, drumming with insects, and the road in front of us shivered in a haze of heat. Whenever we found shade we sheltered in it. At mid-day, when the sun was a blazing yellow ball above our heads, we came to a place where little stalls were set up along the roadside. Some boys who were sitting with a pile of Coke bottles filled with water told us that the bus that went all the way from Dar-Es-Salaam to Arusha should be passing by soon, and that maybe it would stop there to give the passengers a break. A little boy was standing next to a huge pile of smooth green coconuts. He hacked away at them by spearing them with a stick that he held on the ground with his toes. He had a knife between his teeth, and when he saw us he sliced the top off one of the coconuts and handed it to me. I gave it to my mother to drink the juice, and then the boy hacked out the wet flesh for me.

A woman who was cooking little cakes on a pot over a smoky wood fire told her son to give us some orange slices that he was preparing for the passengers.

1 **to prowl** to move around quietly, e.g. when you are hunting – 2 **to splinter** *spalten* – 4 **to creak, scratch, pad, slither, yap** the noises night animals might make when they are prowling – 5 **wingbeats** the beats (esp the noise) of animals with wings

"She going to hospital?" the boy asked, pointing his knife towards my mother. I nodded, squeezing the last juice from the orange, chewing the white pulp to a mush before I spat it out.

"You going on the bus?" his mother called.

"No money," I said. "We have to walk."

"Tchk. She got no walking left in her," the woman said.

"Just resting," Mama said. She closed her eyes and curled up where she was sitting, and the woman clicked her tongue behind her teeth and came over to us, pulling her kanga off her shoulders and making a hood of it to shade Mama's face.

"You got a Baba?" she asked me.

I said nothing. She blew out her cheeks and shook her head. "Poli sikitaba," she said. *I'm sorry.*

Suddenly the boys set up an excited shouting and ran off down the road, waving their arms and skipping, and as the cloud of noisy red dust that was a bus came bumping towards them, they ran back to their piles of bottles and plates of quartered fruits, trays of hard-boiled eggs and maize cakes balanced on their heads, jostling to be seen so people would buy from them. The people in the bus had been sitting for hours, — some of them had been riding on it for over a day. They climbed out, stiff-legged, rubbing their eyes, stretching out their arms, bending their knees. The men went off to one side and the women went to the other, to relieve themselves in the bushes.

Among the passengers were two white women. One wandered away from the bus, and the other called after her, "Don't go too far! There'll be snakes in the bushes!" then turned and came over to buy some of the little hot cakes and sliced mangoes and oranges that the people near us were selling. She had a pale blue cotton scarf wound round her hair and most of

19 **to jostle** ['dʒɒsəl] to push against someone in a crowd – 24 **to relieve os** to urinate – 31 **scarf wound** [waʊnd] **around her hair** piece of cloth on her hair

her face to protect her from the dust of the bus-ride, but before she ate she pulled it away. Her hair shimmered golden-red around her shoulders, like a fire. I would like to touch that hair. She squatted on the ground by me, looking curiously at my mother, who was lying on the ground, not moving, clutching my hand in hers.

"Is she tired?" the woman asked in my language of Swahili.

"No, she's sick," the mango boy told her. "She's going to the hospital to die."

I gave a loud sob then; it jerked out of me like a black fox jumping out of the grass, leaping out of its long hiding place. The woman looked at me, and her face was so soft with pity that I wanted to pick up my mother in my arms and run all the way back to the Bibi's hut with her.

"Where is the hospital?" the woman asked. "Will you go on the bus?"

"No money, Teacha," I whispered shyly in my school English. My throat was clumped up so much with more hidden sobs that the words would hardly sound. She called her friend over and the two women talked to each other so quickly that I couldn't understand a word of it, but I watched them going over to the driver and talking earnestly to him, offering money. He shook his head, and then one of the women took out her purse and offered him more money, and then they were all smiling and nodding towards me. I knew they had bribed him to take us to the hospital.

When the driver was ready to move on, the women helped Mama onto the bus and sat her by the open window, with her kanga over her face to protect her from the dust.

I sat on the floor of the bus, in the gangway, and the big boy who had given up his seat to my mother sat opposite me, laughing as we pitched from side to side on the rutted road. I

4 **to squat** *hocken* – 7 **Swahili** important language, widely spoken in East Africa – 10 **sob** cry *(Schluchzen)* – 10 **to jerk** to move forward suddenly – 25 **to bribe** to give sb money to do sth in order to persuade them to do sth for you, usually something dishonest – 32 **rutted road** road with a lot of holes in it

laughed too, because I was so happy. The long, frightening walk was over and soon, soon now, we would be at the hospital.

The boy told me that during the night the bus had broken down for three hours, and that two men had tried to mend it. In the end the police had come and arrested the owner for having an unroadworthy bus, and taken him off to prison. I laughed again; I hugged myself with joy. If the bus hadn't broken down, we would never have seen it, and the white women wouldn't have paid for us to ride on it. The day was golden again. The oranges boy was wrong. My mother would get better.

6 **unroadworthy bus** a bus that should not be on a road because it is too broken or old

Chapter 4

ROSA

I was sure Mum had forgotten about the adoption child business. She didn't say another word about it, and neither did I. She must have decided it was a bad idea after all. And then, a few days after my birthday, there was a strange woman in our kitchen, drinking tea. She had her hair in long grey plaits and she was wearing flowery trousers and the most beautiful red, green and blue shoes. If there's one thing I love even more than books, it's shoes. I'm going to design them one day, but that's my secret.

"So this is Rosa," she said, and held out her hand, just touching my cheek. I backed away.

"Rosa, this is Miss West," Mum said.

"Molly," the lady said, smiling. "I'm from the adoption society, Rosa."

"Oh," I said. I couldn't keep the disappointment out of my voice. So Mum hadn't forgotten at all. She had been holding it in her head, a private secret, all this time.

I made to run upstairs, but Mum gave me a look that said 'Stay where you are," and then a smile that said, "Please Rosa, don't let me down," and then she really said, "Rosa, get yourself a mug and have a drink of tea with us. And a chocolate biscuit."

I did exactly as I was told. I was a sweet demure child. I ate my biscuit nicely and I answered the Molly lady's questions about school. All I could think was that if the adoption lady saw what a nice girl I was she would realise that Mum didn't need another one.

7 plait [plæt] braid *(Zopf)* – 25 **demure** [dɪˈmjʊə] quiet, serious, well-behaved

We went up to my room, and she cooed over the pile of soft dolls and the poster of Doctor Who and the curtains with the border of teddy bears that Mum had made for me when I was born. I looked at it with a stranger's eyes and knew it was a child's room, not a teenager's. But I was comfortable there. I was safe.

And just when I thought I'd been doing all the right things, she clasped her hands together and said,

"This is such a lovely room. How do you feel about having another bed in here, Rosa? Have you thought about what it will be like to share it with someone?"

There goes my stomach, jerking like a flapping bird. "I don't know," I said.

Much later, when the sky was quite dark outside and I still hadn't put my light on, Mum called up to tell me that tea was ready. She was bright and cheerful; I would almost say she was happy.

"You see, Rosa. About us adopting a child. Imagine what it must be like not to have a mother or a father. To be completely alone in the world. Don't you think it would be lovely to be able to give a home to someone like that?"

It didn't help, being told that. I've lost my dad, too. I don't want a sister or a brother. I never have wanted one. I like it that it's just me and Mum. And if it really happens, this adoption thing, it'll never be just us again. I'll have lost my mum.

1 **to coo** to make a soft sound, *here:* to admire – 2 **Doctor Who** popular children's science fiction TV character (as well as the name of the programme) in the UK – 12 **to jerk** to move suddenly and violently (she is shocked)

Chapter 5

ABELA

Mama slept most of the way to the hospital, her hands fluttering and clasping each other in her lap as if they were talking to one another. When we arrived I woke her up and helped her down the aisle and off the bus. She could hardly stand up, but she clasped the hands of the white woman with the red-gold hair, and thanked her. Then she thanked everyone in her tiny weak voice, nodding and smiling, and so did I. I was so happy that morning.

The white women followed me off the bus.

"Wait child," she said.

I turned round to her. She held out some money to me, and when I shook my head, she pressed it into my hand.

"It's not much, I'm afraid, but you'll need this to buy medicine for your mother. Take it."

I knew she was right. "Thank you, Teacha," I said in English, just as we're taught to do in school.

She smiled. "I'm not a teacher. Just a tourist, enjoying your beautiful country."

I think that's what she said. I know the word tourist means *mgeni*. I don't know what a tourist does though.

I turned away, and she called me back again. "Here, you'll need food," she said. She gave me a handful of sweet doughnuts wrapped in a banana leaf, and some bananas, the ones she had bought at the stop where she met us. "Look after yourself, too. Your mother needs you." The bus driver tooted his horn, revving up the engine, and she hurried back and climbed on, wrapping the blue scarf round her hair and face again. I

6 **aisle** [aɪl] space between two rows of seats in a bus *(Gang)*

strained my eyes, but I couldn't see her as the bus swung round in its cloud of yellow dust. I saw the boy who had given Mama his seat, grinning at me, and I laughed and waved.

"All right now," I said to Mama.

She smiled weakly, and sighed. "Yes, all right now."

The hospital was a long low concrete building, painted white. Crowds of people were milling round it, sick people and their relatives and friends. Some were lying on the ground, some squatting and staring mutely in front of them as if they were looking into their own future and seeing nothing. Some were gossiping as if it was the market, some were sitting apart and alone, waiting, waiting. A sick man arrived propped on a black bicycle; his arms draped over the shoulders of his mother and father, who were supporting him on either side. Behind him trailed his wife and children, carrying clay cooking pots and coloured sheets, bedrolls, little bags of food. Someone shouted, "The water's on!" and there was a rush of women from inside the hospital, carrying the soiled and bloodstained sheets that they had pulled from the beds of their sick relatives. They clustered round the taps, scrubbing the sheets with their fists, jostling each other to get it done before the cold water was turned off again.

Abela and her mother threaded their way into the building. The smell of sweat and sickness was overwhelming. At least it was cooler inside than outside; the electric fans had been switched on at the same time as the water. Rows of iron-railed beds lined the walls, and in them lay the dying, and round them clustered their relatives, feeding them, washing them, stroking them, arguing over their heads. A few had grey, greasy nets slung above the bed, splodged with dead mosquitoes. Every now and then an ululating cry went up, "Lu-lu-lu-lu-lu-lu-lu." It was the cry of grief.

6 **concrete** *Beton* – 7 **to mill round** to wander round (a crowd) – 9 **mute** [mju:t] not saying a word *(stumm)* – 18 **soiled** dirty – 20 **to scrub** to rub hard (usually done with a brush) – 23 **to thread** [θred] to move slowly and carefully – 24 **overwhelming** very strong – 32 **grief** extreme sadness, especially after a death

Those who had chosen to go home to die were carried out in the arms of their relatives. They were as thin and weak as baby birds. The weary nurses walked from bed to bed, doing what they could. They wore immaculate starched headdresses like white crowns on their heads. One of them sang, in a deep, croaky voice, as she trudged around the ward. It was as if it was only the singing that was keeping her going.

And into this stinking hellhole Abela and her mother walked. If she thought her mother had the strength, Abela would have turned round and taken her home again, walked through the sticky days and the lonely nights with her; anything rather than leave her here. As it was, she knew that all her mother wanted was to lie down and sleep. She watched a nurse throwing a stained sheet off an empty bed, and steered her mother towards it. Her mother sank down gratefully onto the filthy mattress and smiled up at Abela.

"Good girl," she whispered, like a sigh of wind. "You go home now."

"No," said Abela firmly. "I'm staying with you, Mama. I'm going to make you better."

Her mother eyes glistened. She turned her head away and fell asleep.

Abela sat on the edge of the bed and watched the bewildering bustle of the ward. So many people. So much noise. She saw a boy of her own age come weaving in and out of the lines of beds with a live hen clutched in his hands. He was trying to catch the attention of one of the white-crowned nurses, but she seemed to ignore him. The hen clucked and squawked in shrill indignation, pecking the boy's fingers. At last the nurse turned round. Her eyes were nearly shut with weariness. The boy thrust the hen towards her.

3 **weary** very tired – 4 **immaculate** [ɪˈmækjələt] very clean – 4 **starched** *gestärkt* – 6 **croaky** *here:* not clear – 6 **to trudge** [trʌdʒ] to step heavily or slowly or lazily – 6 **ward** *Krankenstation* – 14 **stained** dirty – 15 **filthy** very dirty – 21 **to glisten** [glɪsən] to shine and look oily – 23 **bewildering** [bɪˈwɪldərɪŋ] **bustle** [ˈbʌsəl] confusing activity – 29 **indignation** [ɪndɪgˈneɪʃen] feeling of anger and surprise – 31 **to thrust** to throw

"Please can I buy medicine for my father?" he asked.

The nurse shook her head. "You'd do better to take your kuku outside and cook it. Make a nice tasty stew for your Baba instead."

"Please," the boy begged. "Mama said we haven't any money for medicine."

"I said no." The nurse walked on past him. "Take your hen away."

Abela remembered the money that the woman from the bus had given her. She ran after the nurse and tugged her arm. "I've got money," she said. "Some medicine for my Mama and some for his Baba. Real money."

She held out her hand. The coins were hot and wet in her palm, she'd been clutching them so tightly.

The nurse clicked her tongue impatiently. "Money or hens, mangoes or bicycles, they're no use, child. Nothing is any more. We haven't got any medicines left. We ran out of them two weeks ago."

Abela stared at her, unbelieving. They had come all this way for help – surely there was something her mother could be given to ease her? The medicine man in the village would have found something for her, a weed or a herb, a coloured potato, the juice of crushed insects, anything rather than send her away with nothing.

"Can I pay for a doctor to see her?"

"No doctors here," the nurse said. "They've all moved on, or died. Your money is useless, little one, wherever you got it from. You can't even eat it. The only thing you can buy here is coffins." She squatted down, moved at last by pity for the desperate child. "Go home. Take your Mama home. That's best. There's nothing we can do for her."

Abela turned away from her, more upset by the hopelessness in the nurse's eyes than she had been by her earlier harshness.

3 **stew** cooked meal: a thick soup made with vegetables and sometimes meat – 14 **palm** [pɑ:m] the flat, front side of your hand – 22 **weed or herb** *(Un)Kraut* – 29 **coffin** large box in which dead people are placed before they are buried – 30 **desperate** ['desprət] willing to do or try anything because things are so bad

She hooked up a corner of her kanga to make a pocket, and tied the coins into it. She went back to her mother and sat by her, bleak and cold now, the joy of the morning all gone. The woman who was washing her daughter in the next bed called over to her, "Medicine truck will be coming tomorrow, that's what I've heard. Why don't you get your mother some water? They'll be turning it off soon, and there'll be no more today." She handed Abela a Coca-Cola bottle without a cap.

Abela was glad to have something to do. She ran out to the tap in the yard and waited in the queue, and at last her turn came. The bottle was only half-full when the trickle of water stopped. She saw the boy who had been talking to the nurse standing listlessly, still clutching the hen. The bird squirmed in his hands, tapping his fingers with its beak.

"The medicine truck is coming tomorrow," she told him. "It'll be all right then."

He looked at her blankly.

When her mother woke up, Abela tried to feed her with bits of broken biscuit and crushed banana, but she hardly ate anything.

"You," she gestured to Abela. "You have it."

"No, Mama. You eat it."

"You need it to keep strong," her mother said. She closed her eyes and turned her face away. "Be strong, my Abela."

When night fell, sudden and full, some of the people outside the hospital lit their little paraffin lamps and built fires out of sticks, balanced their cooking pots on three stones over the flames, and heated up chicken bones and beans or whatever bits of food they had brought with them. Some rolled themselves up by their fires to sleep. Others swarmed into the ward and stretched out on the floor between the beds. Abela climbed into bed with her mother, wrapped her arms round her, and slept deeply from utter weariness.

3 **bleak** sad, hopeless – 10 **tap** *Wasserhahn* – 10 **queue** [kjuː] line of people – 11 **trickle of water** water drops – 13 **to squirm** [skwɜːm] to twist one's body, usually when you are uncomfortable or want to get away – 33 **utter weariness** extreme tiredness

Chapter 6

ABELA

I stayed with Mama in that hospital all that week, but no medicine truck came, no doctors. Mama grew so weak that she couldn't do anything for herself. There were no sheets for her bed. I used some of my money to buy two cotton kangas from the family of a woman who had died, and used them in turn. Every day when the water came on I would roll Mama over and pull away the one she was lying on, and spread the other one out as carefully as I could, with no lumps and creases to hurt her. Then I followed the other women and girls to the taps and scrubbed the soiled kanga as best as I could, but they never came clean again. I spread it out in the sun to dry, ready for the next day. Then I took some water in the Coke bottle and washed my mother down with it, and last of all, gave her some to drink.

Sometimes people gave me bits of food from their pots. Somebody gave me a coconut and pierced it for me, and I trickled the sweet milk into Mama's mouth. I could see that she loved it. I sat on somebody's grating stool and shredded the coconut meat, and the owner of the stool boiled it with her sweet potatoes and filled my coconut shell with it for our meal. They were like a village, those people outside the hospital, and the boy with the hen and I and other children who were on their own wandered from group to group, grateful for any scraps that people gave us. An old man with a beard like a cloud of froth called me over every day to give me a handful of his cooked maize. I got to know their names, and it was like another life, and I would be living there forever.

10 **lump** *Klumpen* – 10 **crease** [kri:s] *Falte* – 20 **grating stool** *Hocker zum Mahlen* – 26 **scraps** leftover pieces of food – 27 **froth** foam

But after the first week, Mama stopped eating or drinking. She could only stare at me, and her eyes were so fevered and burning that I wanted to close them for her so I couldn't see her pain. The only thing she said to me after that first week was this:

"Be strong. Be a strong girl, my Abela."

I couldn't sleep in her bed any longer. She burned like a fire. I slept on the floor at the side of it, and when I didn't sleep, I listened to the sighing and groaning, the weeping round the ward, and I was no longer afraid of any of the noises. They were only the sounds of sick people. "One day, I'll learn how to make people better," I said out loud. "And I'll come back and make you all well again."

I went out next day as usual when the water came on. It was like a song, and I knew the words off by heart. Change kanga, wash it, fill bottle, wash Mama, find food. But when I came back, the singing nurse was standing by Mama's bed. She was still singing, her own low, deep song like a flowing river, but the white wings of her head-dress hid her face from me. When she heard me coming she turned towards me and her eyes told me everything. I was filled with a cold, terrible, terrified dread. And my song came from me, from deep inside, and there is no stopping it when the grief is on us; it's the sound we make when someone has given up their soul at last; the song of death.

For three days Abela lay under her mother's bed, refusing to move. The nurses gave up trying to make her go away; they were too busy. After a time they stopped noticing her. When at last she crawled out she saw that there was a stranger in Mama's bed now, someone who looked like Mama but wasn't her, someone with arms like sticks and eyes as bright as burning coals. Abela went outside slowly, shielding her eyes against the blinding light of the sun. This hospital that had been like

31 **to shield** to protect

a whole world to her for weeks on end was an alien place now. She didn't belong here any more. She had to go home. The water was running again, and she filled up her plastic bottle at the tap, knowing dimly that she would need it on her journey. She must walk towards the morning sun, she knew that too. She knew nothing else. She was numb and cold and deeply afraid. She set off along the road towards the blinding orange sun, then stood aside as a van trundled towards her. There was a shout behind her and she saw people running to meet the van, yelling, cheering, banging on the sides, holding out their hands.

"Wait, wait, please wait!" Abela saw a boy break away from the crowd round the van and come running towards her, waving his arms in the air. It was the chicken boy. She waited, staring blankly at his excitement.

"Come back!" he shouted, as he drew near her. "It's the medicine van! The medicines have come!"

Medicine. She frowned, searching deep inside herself to find the meaning of the word, or the significance of the boy's excitement. He had reached her now, and he stood in front of her, gasping for breath, his hand stretched out towards her.

"Money," the boy said again. "For my father. To make him better."

She lifted up the corner of her kanga and untied the knot she had made in it, very slowly, because her fingers were stiff and numb and seemed not to belong to her at all, and then she handed the boy the coins that the white woman had given her. Without a word the boy turned and ran away, back to the van, back to the voices of the earth, the voices of hope.

Abela stumbled on towards the sun. When it was directly over her head she found some shade and slept a little, and then walked on with the sun behind her. Sometimes people came out of the trees towards her, slipping past her and out of her

4 **dimly** *here:* not exactly – 8 **to trundle** to move slowly but steadily

life as silently as they had come; ghost people, the people of dreams, the silent ones.

The sun had gone completely now. Fireflies danced like bright blue flames, then darted away. The sky was brilliant with clusters of stars, and the moon blazed in its own white brightness. Abela walked quickly, listening in her head to her mother's pretty blue voice. Then suddenly the song stopped, and Abela froze. There came another sound, and Abela knew that it was not inside her head but was part of the living darkness around her. The sound was stealthy and smooth, feet padding on crinkled stalks, strong bodies pushing canes aside, swift now, and purposeful.

That was the night she saw the lions.

I knew what they were before I even saw them. I didn't know whether to run away or to stay still. I wanted to lie down and wait. My bones were so tired that I just wanted to sink down onto the ground and sleep. I no longer knew where I was walking to or from, or why. I just wanted to sleep. Then the moon glided out from behind a tree and I saw the lions, and they saw me. There was one male and two lionesses. They were as still as statues, and they looked as if they were made of gold. Their eyes gleamed in the moonlight. *Please, please, holy God who comes with the priest to our church, don't let them kill me. Please. You have already taken my mother and my father. Please let me live.* These were the words that were beating in my head like drums, so fast that they weren't words at all, so loud that they drowned my heartbeats and the tremble of my breath. And my mother's voice was singing through them, *be strong, my Abela, be strong.* I felt her standing by my side. I felt my father standing behind me, with his hands on my shoulders. I was as still as they were, as silent, as watchful.

4 **to dart** to jump away quickly and suddenly – 5 **to blaze** to shine very brightly – 10 **stealthy** ['stelθi] (as though the lion was) moving quietly and secretly – 11 **crinked stalks** *zerknitterte Stängel* – 11 **cane** thin stick – 12 **swift** quick – 12 **purposeful** ['pɜːpəsfəl] having a clear aim *(Ziel)*

And at last the lions left me. They turned their heads and padded away, shimmering black and gold through the trees.

I was alone again. The huge silence of the night wrapped itself around me. The massive stars gleamed down on me like eyes. *Thank you,* I whispered. I let my voice trail out of me, and there was no answering roar. I was quite safe. I began to walk again, quickly this time, and then when I reached the road I began to run. I had thought I wanted to die, but when I saw the lions, I knew I wanted to live.

By the end of the next day Abela was back in her grandmother's house. There was no need to tell Bibi what had happened. The old woman held out her arms to her and rocked her, and they wept together. She gave her some soup and then wrapped her up in her arms again and they slept together on the mattress. It was a whole day before Abela woke up again. She lay listening to the village sounds outside the hut; children laughing, hens clucking, the steady chip, chip, chip of someone chopping wood. Everything was right again. Nothing was right.

She ran outside. Her grandmother was bent double, chipping a log to make kindling for the cooking fire. She was too weak to swing the axe like Mama used to do. Chip, chip, chip went the axe, sending little white splinters like sparks into the air. When she saw Abela she straightened up slowly, easing her back with one bony hand, wiping away the sweat from her brow with the other.

"Bibi, where is she?" Abela asked, though, of course, she knew. Her sister's little sleeping mat had gone. They had lost Nyota, their little star.

I don't know why God did this to me. He has taken nearly everything that belongs to me, and I am so afraid because I don't know where it will stop. Perhaps my grandmother will be

5 **to trail out** to come out slowly – 17 **to chop** to cut – 19 **bent double** *vorn über gebeugt* – 20 **kindling** easily burnable material used to start a fire

the next, but she says no, she is too old to die of this sickness, she will die of something else.

"And me?" I hardly dared ask such a question. Fright was fluttering in my throat like a butterfly.

Grandmother Bibi shook her head. "Your Mama and Baba were not ill when you were born, they were healthy and strong. But by the time they were waiting for Nyota to be born, they were already very sick themselves. So the baby had no chance."

"No chance?"

"No. That baby had no chance to live."

I stared into the pile of chippings that my grandmother had made. I have heard of a baby who was born with no sight. I have even heard of a baby born with no arms. But I have never heard of a baby born with no chance. And this was a new thing for me to think about; to live or to die, to be sick or to be healthy, was all a matter of chance? Could this be true?

4 **to flutter** *flattern* – 13 **sight** eyesight, the ability to see

Chapter 7

ROSA

"Molly's coming round after school. Mum said.

I wore my sequin shoes again, and they were much admired. Molly told me about a pair of patent leather shoes she had been given when she was my age, and how she would shine them with the sleeve of her cardigan till she could see her face in them. She asked me about skating, and whether I'd learned any new moves since she last saw me. Fool that I was, and a born show-off, I demonstrated the knee bend, sliding about in my sparklers across the kitchen floor, which made her laugh and cough.

And then, just when she had crossed the enemy line and had become a friend, she said, "If we do find a sister for you, would you like to teach her to skate?"

I stopped immediately, in mid-flight, one knee bent and the other leg stretched behind me, perfectly balanced and frozen solid now as if the kitchen was full of ice, as if I was carved out of ice, as if she and Mum were two ice maidens.

From somewhere deep inside the heart of a glacier, Molly said, "Rosa, you're not really happy about the idea of adopting, are you?"

I was too stiff and cold with ice to say anything.

"We need to have a proper talk about this. I'm trying to imagine how I would have felt if it had been me, if my mum had wanted to introduce another girl into the family when I was your age. Is it because Mum would like it to be a girl of

4 **sequin** small piece of shiny metal – 5 **patent** ['peɪtənt] **leather** shiny leather – 7 **cardigan** jacket made of wool – 11 **sparklers** *here:* sparkling *(glitzernd)* shoes – 17 **frozen solid** absolutely still and not moving – 18 **to carve** *schnitzen* – 19 **ice maiden** beautiful and graceful girl that lives in cold places – 20 **glacier** ['glæsiə] *Gletscher*

around your age? Would you be happier if we were talking about a little boy, a brother for you?"

"I hate boys," came my stiff, frozen robot voice.

"Or a baby."

"Babies stink of poo." I said.

Mum sighed, a deep, hopeless sigh, and I suddenly realised that I was the one with power now, not Molly, not Mum. I could make this thing not happen. They were waiting for me to say yes, and all I had to do was to say no. And when I realised that, I felt strong, my ice melted away from me and I went calmly upstairs to my room, put my magic twinkling shoes in their box, and started my Maths homework.

I could hear Mum and Molly talking, their voices rolling and pattering and running together like rainwater. I wasn't upset any more, I wasn't angry. I just got on with what I wanted to do. No need to be cute and friendly and too nice to need a sister. After a bit, as I knew she would, Molly came up and knocked on my door. I didn't answer but she came in anyway and sat on the end of my bed. She tweaked her plait over her shoulder.

"Your mother and I have decided that I won't come again for a bit."

Hmm. I finished my Maths problem, closed the book, and clicked my pen so the nib retracted.

"Not unless you want me to," Molly went on. "Sharing your home with someone, adopting someone into it, is a really big decision, and the whole family really needs to want to do it. You're not at all sure about this. That's fine. Some children of your age feel puzzled. They think, why should Mum want another child, when she's got me?"

My breath gave a sharp snatch. I stared out of the window. The street was dark. The street lamp was a hazy orange blur.

5 **poo** *(inf) Kot* – 11 **to twinkle** to shine (like a star) – 16 **cute** *(inf)* pretty and attractive – 19 **to tweak** *here:* to place in a careful and graceful way – 23 **the nib** the pointed end part of a pen – 23 **to retract** to move back – 31 **the lamp was a hazy blur** the light is not clear

"Sometimes they feel jealous, " Molly went on quietly. "They think, doesn't my Mum love me? Aren't I enough for her?"

Just under my eyelids the tears were beginning to brim.

"Or they feel angry and upset."

Then she was quiet for ages, and so was I. I could hear next door's dog padding down the entry, his paws scratching, whining at the gate to be let out.

That was when Molly gave me the book. It was a large hard-backed book with pink and blue stripes across it. I opened it up. The pages were completely blank, apart from faint grey lines. Molly rummaged in her bag again and gave me a gold plastic pen with *zebra* written on the side.

"It might be a good idea to write all your thoughts down here," she said. "Just absolutely everything that comes into your head. You know, about your feelings, about your mum, about me if you want. You don't have to show it to anyone. Or you could show it to me one day, if you want to, and if you want me to come again. Some children write about their hobbies and their friends and their school too, but that's only when they decide that they want to adopt someone and they want to tell them about their family."

I stroked the book. "Can I write about skating, even though we might not adopt anyone?"

"If you want. Gosh, that would be a lovely thing to write about." Molly smiled and stood up. "You'd enjoy that. But Rosa, only write the truth. OK? It isn't a storybook. OK?"

That night, I started to write in my book. I thought for ages about where to start it, and then I remembered the day Mum told me that she wanted us to adopt a sister. That was the day I had realised that I didn't know Mum properly, that there was something about her that I didn't know and that I didn't understand. But I wasn't ready to go there yet. Instead, I wrote about skating.

3 **tears brim** her eyes are full of tears: she is about to cry – 10 **faint** not clear

I love skating, more than anything else in the world. Mum and I are learning together. We go to the skating rink every Saturday morning, and we take the same class. We're just about as good as each other. I can go backwards, I can go in circles, I can criss-cross. I love the music, which makes me want to dance and sing, and the sounds of the skates freeshing on the ice. I love the rush of excitement I feel when I try a new move, and try and try again because it's too hard at first, testing out which way to tilt my foot, inside edge, outside edge, and then find out I can do it. Most of all, I love it because it's something my mum and I do together.

Once I'd started I just couldn't stop, it was pouring out of me, a river of words. At first everything came out in the wrong order, just as I remembered it. But now, I've reached the day where Molly gave me the striped book. I think I want to keep on writing in it. I'm trying to write the exact truth. And this is my true thought for today. I'm going to ask Mum why she wants another daughter.

9 **to tilt** to move to the side slightly

Chapter 8

ABELA

A month passed, and Abela slept a lot, cried a lot, dragged herself to school when she could. She kept thinking she could hear Mama singing, or the little whimpering cry that Nyota used to make when she was waking up, or her father's deep rolling laughter. But the little house was empty of sound, except for Bibi's low voice persuading her to eat, drink, get up, give her some help. It never occurred to Abela that her grandmother was as steeped in grief as she was for the three losses to her family. Bibi just kept going, and tried to keep the world moving for Abela.

One day when she came home from school, she found her grandmother making little maize cakes, special occasion cakes, on the griddle over the charcoal stove.

"I have had a message to say that your uncle is coming home!" Bibi's eyes were dancing with smiles. "Yes, your Uncle Thomas has come home from Europe, and he has a surprise for you."

"I don't know Uncle Thomas," Abela said.

"Well, you do, but you were only four or five when he went away to Europe. He fell in love with a rich tourist who gave him the money to go to her country, and I thought he would never come home again." She said the word *mgeni*, which meant tourist, with a mixture of pride and contempt. She did not like them. When they climbed off the bus to stretch their legs they stared and took photographs, they wandered round the village and peered in the huts as if they owned the place. Abela

3 **to drag os** *sich schleppen* – 8 **to persuade** [pəˈsweɪd] to make sb decide to do sth – 10 **to be steeped in grief** to have a lot of grief *(sadness)* – 25 **contempt** *Verachtung*

thought about the lady tourist with the hair like flames that she had met on the way to the hospital, and said nothing about it.

"Why has he come home from Europe?" she asked. To her, Europe was one big place, one massive world where many white people lived. Everybody who lived in Europe was rich. Why would Uncle Thomas want to come home again?

Bibi shrugged. She flipped the maize cakes over on the skillet. "He wasn't allowed to stay any longer. They threw him out, his friend said." she announced dramatically, as if that made him a hero.

Abela stared into the charcoal fire, frowning. She dimly remembered her uncle now. He was a bully, she remembered. He used to shout a lot at her mother, and sometimes he hit her. He used to tease Abela and chase her into the monkey woods until she cried, and then he would make his voice squawk like a hen with laughter. She used to be afraid of him.

"Well, he's coming home. I've had a message to say he will be on the bus tonight. All the way from Dar-Es-Salaam! He'll be tired, he'll be hungry, he'll be dirty. Don't expect much from him tonight. He's bringing someone with him. And he has a surprise for you."

"For me?"

"There, now you want to see him, don't you? He's a good boy. He doesn't forget his old mother and his little niece."

When the cakes were made, Bibi shook out the bedroll ready for Uncle Thomas to sleep on. She and Abela would sleep together on Mama's bedroll, she said. Plenty of room. And the guest would sleep on Abela's bedroll. Bibi was like a girl again, excited and laughing at the thought of seeing her son after five years, and her excitement affected Abela. She magicked what the surprise might be in her head. Maybe he had brought her some pencils from Europe.

8 **skillet** ['skɪlɪt] frying pan – 12 **bully** ['bʊli] sb who uses his strength to frighten sb who is weaker – 14 **to tease** [ti:z] to laugh at – 18 **Dar-Es-Salaam** [ˌdɑ:resˌsə'lɑ:m] – 30 **to magic** *here:* to imagine

When the time came to meet the bus they strolled together through the compound and up past the schoolhouse to the road, Bibi shouting out to her friends that Thomas was coming home. The fireflies blazed a blue trail for them. Food stalls were being set up on trellis tables along the roadside to greet the bus passengers, paraffin lamps lit, music playing from someone's portable radio. Even though this happened every time the bus passed by the village, it felt as if everyone had turned out that night to meet Uncle Thomas.

The bus was five hours late. It didn't matter. That was quite normal. Abela curled up on the ground and slept. She opened her eyes to see a white woman looking down at her, the light of the lamps flickering across her face and making her long pale yellow hair gleam.

"What a pretty child, Thomas. Is this Bella?"

Recognising her name among the English words, Abela sat up with a start and struggled to her feet. Bibi was hugging Uncle Thomas, who was dressed in strange trousers and shoes, not blue jeans like the men in the village, not shorts like the tourists.

"Look at these smart clothes!" Bibi clucked in admiration. "You must be a rich man these days!"

Thomas put his arm round his friend's waist. She swung her hair and gleamed a smile at him. "This is Susie," he said. "Say hello, Abela. Say it in English."

Abela rubbed the palms of her hands together nervously. "Morning, Teacha!" she said.

"Well, it's not morning, it's nearly midnight," Susie laughed. White, white, thought Abela. Oh, her voice is as white as the moon. I have never heard a lovely moon-white quiet-soft voice like that before. "And I'm certainly not a teacher. Not clever enough! Not bossy enough!" She crouched down to Abela. "Do you speak much English, Bella?"

4 **to blaze a trail** to make a bright path – 5 **trellis** *here:* wooden – 7 **even though** although – 14 **to gleam** to shine – 23 **waist** *Taille* – 32 **to crouch** [kraʊtʃ] *hinhocken*

Abela bit her lip and scratched the ground with her big toe. "A little bit," she whispered. She glanced shyly up at her grandmother. "Teacha say me I best in school." Then she burrowed her face into Bibi's side.

"You'd better be," Susie said. "Because I don't speak one word of your language. Oh, yes I do! One word – jambo! That means hello, doesn't it? I love that word. Jambo! Jambo everybody!"

Abela struggled to stay awake while the bean stew and the maize cakes were prepared. The sky hung like a black tent over them. Susie and Thomas sat outside the hut with little lamps glowing around them to keep away the mosquitoes. Huge moths fluttered round the lamps and Susie flapped her hands at them. Her rings sparkled like stars. When Bibi proudly served out the bowls of food, Susie said she was too tired to eat.

"Can we go and sleep now?" she asked. "I'm sorry, I can't keep my eyes open, Thomas."

Thomas waved his hand towards his mother's hut. "Go ahead."

"In there? I can't sleep in there! Isn't there a hotel?"

"Not unless you want to walk about fifty miles."

Bibi smiled and nodded, understanding nothing except that her guest was too tired to eat.

Susie peered into the hut, and backed out again. "I won't sleep in there," she said firmly. "It's too dark, and it stinks of smoke, and there's no room."

"Oh, for heaven's sake!" Thomas snapped.

"Isn't there a proper house anywhere?"

"Stop whining! If you're tired, sleep in there. If you're not, sit here and wait for the lions."

Susie yelped and groped her way into the blackness of the mud hut, and Bibi followed her and showed her the bedroll that she was to sleep on. Susie covered herself up with the blanket and went straight to sleep. Abela lay on the roll that

4 **to burrow** ['bʌrəʊ] to bury, hide – 23 **to peer** to look closely (when you can't see sth well) – 30 **to yelp** to let out a short cry – 30 **to grope** to try to find sth that you cannot see

used to be Mama's and looked across at her, at the beautiful pale yellow hair, at the white face like a sleeping moon, just lit by the glow from outside.

The fire under the cooking pot died down, the hut was in darkness, and Bibi and Uncle Thomas talked on, sitting just outside the hut in the starlight.

As soon as Abela woke up, she remembered that Susie was there. She sat up and looked across to where the pink morning light lit up Susie's face and hair. She could see the fine golden down on her cheeks, and the flutter of her pale eyelashes. Bibi was stoking the stove to heat up the maize porridge for breakfast, and a sudden gust of smoke drenched the air. Susie woke up, coughing. She blundered outside, gasping and spluttering, breathing in the fresh air.

"How can you live in there, with all that smoke?" she shouted. "I smell like a kipper, Thomas."

Thomas stretched and rolled himself over. "You'll get used to it," he called back. "Don't make a fuss."

But Abela jumped out of her bedroll and ran to the red plastic bucket of water that Bibi had carried from the well the day before, balancing it on her head the way all the women did, never spilling a drop all the long way home. She scooped some out with a coconut shell and carried it over to where Susie sat, still gasping, away from the house.

Susie shook her head. "You're a good girl," she said. "But I daren't drink this water. I'll get typhoid or something. I've got some in a bottle somewhere in my bag."

"It very good water," Abela said, understanding a little. She sipped some and offered the shell bowl again. "Mm, good for Susie. Nini nini pende. Very nice."

11 **porridge** ['pɒrɪdʒ] oats *(Haferflocken)* cooked in milk or water – 12 **gust of smoke** sudden movement of smoke – 12 **to drench** *here:* to fill the air – 16 **kipper** smoked herring – 18 **to make a fuss** to become annoyed – 26 **typhoid** ['taɪfɔɪd] *Typhus* – 29 **to sip** to drink slowly *(nippen)*

Uncle Thomas strolled over to them, his shirt loose over his strange trousers. He was carrying a plastic bottle of water and a bowl of maize porridge. He squatted down beside them. "What do you think of Abela? Is she good enough? Smile Abela. Smile for Susie."

Abela bit her lip, wishing he would go away and leave her with Susie.

"She's just lost her mother, poor kid. Why should she smile?" Susie said. "She's lovely. Anyway, what do you mean, good enough? Good enough for what?"

Thomas didn't answer. He told Abela to fetch some porridge for herself and Susie, and laughed at the face Susie pulled when she tasted it.

"How old are you, Abela?" he asked suddenly, in English.

"I think I nine year old," Abela answered proudly.

"She's little for her age," he commented. He dug his fingers into Abela's shoulders, turning her round and sizing her up as if she were a calf he might be buying from the market. He cupped her face in his hands. "Skinny as a rat. Open your mouth," he ordered. "Baby teeth, still."

She pulled away from him, her eyes stinging, and he laughed and tweaked her nose playfully.

"Are you going to school today?" he asked.

Abela nodded. She didn't want to. She wanted to stay and look at Susie all day.

"Take Susie with you, show her round. She'd like to meet your teacher. She can talk some new English words to you kids. And afterwards, take her to the market." He fished in his pockets and tossed some coins on the ground. "Buy your grandmother some decent cakes, and a kuku, a nice fat chicken. And get yourself a nice new kanga to wear at my wedding. You too, Susie." He added in English. "I want you to wear a kanga tomorrow."

18 **to cup** *here:* to take – 21 **to sting** to hurt – 29 **to toss** *(inf)* to throw

As soon as they were out of sight, Thomas called his mother over. "Has the kid been to the clinic recently? Have they tested her for Aids?"

"She's clear," Bibi said. "We're both clear, thanks be to Jesus Christ our Lord."

"She's had all the tests? You're quite sure? She's had injections? You got the papers to show me?" he demanded.

"They gave me something. How do I know what it says?" His mother went into the hut, lifted up the bedroll that Thomas had been sleeping on, and brought out a document. He scrutinised it carefully and then folded it and put it in his back pocket.

"How do you think you're going back to that place, England? Tell me about this plan of yours," his mother said.

Thomas laughed. He took some coins from his pocket and jugged them up and down in the palm of his hand. "In a few days, Susie has to return to England. She's already bought her ticket, so she has to go then. But when she goes back, she'll be married to me." He tiptoed a dance around his mother, a stately Western dance, jingling the coins like bells and making her smile. "I get the documents tomorrow. Then I just have to apply to join my wife. That's what my plan is."

"I don't understand. What documents? All documents, papers, this and that, passports, I don't understand any of it." The old woman flapped her hand in front of her face as if she were flapping flies away. "And how can you get married tomorrow? Tomorrow is not the priest's day for coming here."

"Priest!" Thomas laughed. "I don't need a priest!" He drew a wad of bank notes out of his pocket. "This is all I need. American dollars. More valuable than English sterling. I can buy anything I want with these, if I give them to the right people. I can buy a marriage certificate. I can buy a paper to say we have a child."

"Your child was never born. You told me."

10 **to scrutinize** ['skru:tɪnaɪz] to examine carefully – 15 **to jug** *here:* to move – 18 **to tiptoe** to walk quietly on your toes – 28 **wad** *(inf)* [wɒd] big pile – 29 **valuable** ['væljuəbəl] worth a lot of money

"No problem. I can buy a certificate to say I have a daughter. A birth certificate. The English government won't keep me away from my wife and child. I can buy a passport for her."

"For her? For whom?" His mother sat down suddenly on the little stool she used for shredding coconut. She knew, of course she knew, whom he was talking about, but her quaking heart would not allow her to say so.

"For Abela Mbisi," he bent down to her, smiling, and whispered the words in her ear.

"My Abela?"

"Your Abela! My dead sister's orphan child, in need of a mother and father. What kind of a life will she have here? How long can you look after her? When I have these papers, it will say that Abela is my daughter, Susie's daughter. It will say she is seven years old. That will sound better – Susie's only twenty-five. So, Abela goes home to England with her mother at the end of the week. And I will apply for immigration papers because I have a wife and child in England. It's so simple. You have a clever son, mother." He went down on his knees and put his arms round her. "You want this for me, don't you? You want it for Abela. A better life, away from all this poverty and disease? When I'm back in England I can get a job. I know how to earn good money, very, very good money. And everything I earn I'll send to you. Half."

"Tchk! Money! What do I want with money!" His mother wiped his arms away. "I won't let you take Abela away from me. She's all I've got."

Thomas stood up again and shook the dust from the knees of his trousers. "And you're a selfish old cow. In England she'll have shoes on her feet and good food in her belly. She'll sleep in a big house and go to a proper school. She'll get a good education. She'll get good medical care. I'm offering her the chance of a lifetime. Ma, listen to me. I know about these

2 **birth certificate** ['bɜːθsəˌtɪfɪkət] *Geburtsurkunde* – 5 **to shred** to cut up – 6 **to quake** to shake *(zittern)* – 11 **orphan** child without parents – 29 **selfish** only caring about os

things. There are other little girls that I have found homes for – I know nice English families who want little girls like Abela to help them in their big house. There's plenty of money for you and me." He rubbed his thumb and first finger together. "And plenty good life for my brother's child. Who are you to turn it down for her?"

"She won't want to leave me," Bibi muttered. "She loves her grandmother."

"She loves Susie already. You saw them, hand in hand. They're getting on like a house on fire."

"A house on fire!" His mother was horrified. "What a terrible thought."

The next day, Abela wore her new yellow and black kanga and Susie wore a red and green one that Abela had chosen for her in the market. They walked solemnly behind Uncle Thomas to the next village, where they met two strangers in a concrete schoolhouse. One of the men talked in rapid Kiswahili, which Thomas translated for Susie. The other man, glistening with sweat, sat at a desk and wrote meticulously on three pieces of paper. Abela noticed that he didn't use a pencil, but a black pen with a gold nib. From time to time he shook it to make the ink flow. When he had finished writing, he asked Uncle Thomas and Susie for their signatures. Then he produced a camera and ushered them outside, and took photographs, one of the group together, one of Thomas on his own, one of Susie with Abela, one of Thomas with Abela, and one with Abela on her own.

"Smile!" Uncle Thomas shouted. "Look happy! It's my wedding day." He looked at the other men and squawked with laughter. Abela was too frightened to smile. Nothing like this had ever happened to her before. What happened to her when the camera was pointed at her like that? She had heard that it

4 **thumb** [θʌm] part of your hand *(Daumen)* – 7 **to mutter** to speak in a low voice – 15 **solemn** ['sɒləm] very serious – 17 **Kiswahili** same as Swahili, a major language spoken in East Africa – 19 **meticulous** very exact, precise – 21 **ink** *Tinte*

took your soul away, to have a photograph taken. She clutched her arms across her chest, holding her soul in place.

"That should cover all possibilities," Abela heard the man with the camera say to her uncle. "That's done now."

Both men shook hands with Thomas and Susie and pronounced them married.

"Is that it?" Susie asked doubtfully. "Is that how you do it here?"

"It is when you're in a hurry," Thomas told her. He kissed her hand, which was melting with sweat by now. "We'll do it again when I'm home in England with you. You can have a church wedding and a white dress like a fairy, and a taxi to the church, and a big party." He spoke to her as if she were a little girl deserving treats for being good.

Susie frowned, knowing that that was unlikely too. Her parents didn't like Thomas at all. They'd met him twice, when they had visited her in London some years ago, and they had told her then to keep clear of him.

So she didn't tell her parents when Thomas was deported from England because he had stayed without a visa, an illegal immigrant. She was very much in love with him. She couldn't bear to be without him, so she agreed to go with him to Tanzania to be married. She simply told her parents that she was going on a long holiday because she needed a break from her work. She didn't tell them, either, that she was going to have his baby, or that she had miscarried at five months. She thought she was going to lose Thomas then, too, because he seemed to lose interest in her at that point. But coming to Tanzania with him had brought them closer together. And then when he said he wanted to marry her, all she could think of was that he loved her after all. What would her mother think now of this bleak little ceremony in a concrete hut, in a language she didn't understand, with only a little girl as a witness? She

1 **to clutch** to hold sth tightly – 15 **unlikely** not probable *(unwahrscheinlich)* – 26 **to miscarry** to give birth to a dead child – 33 **witness** *here: Trauzeuge*

watched Thomas as he brought out some bank notes and handed them to the men.

“Is that usual too?” she asked, doubtful again.

“I’ve told you, we’re in a hurry. And these men have come a long way. You don’t expect them to do it for nothing, do you? If you didn’t have to go back to work we would have had more time. But how could I let you go back to England without marrying you? I love you too much for that.”

He kissed her then, and Abela, hovering behind Susie, lowered her eyes and smiled. She still didn’t like her uncle much, but she already loved his princess bride. She didn’t know yet about the plan to send her to England. Her grandmother was too upset to tell her. Her uncle wasn’t sure that her forged passport would be ready in time, so he said nothing. And as for Susie; she simply didn’t know.

After the wedding, Uncle Thomas went off somewhere with the two men. He told Susie he was going to sort out his documents. The three men walked away, laughing, Thomas in the middle with his arms over the shoulders of the other two. Abela saw them heading for the local pombe bar where a strong beer made of coconut palm sap was sold, but she said nothing. So they walked back to Bibi’s house hand in hand. Boys tending their goats in an overgrown cemetery shouted greetings to them. High above their heads men were gathering bananas in the trees, singing loudly. Monkeys jabbered a shrill chorus. A laughing jackass cackled down at them. It was a day like any other day, but it should have been a special day. Abela could sense that Susie was sad; she wanted to make her smile again.

“Tell me English,” she said.

3 **doubtful** ['daʊtfəl] disbelieving – 9 **to hover** ['hɒvə] to wait in an expectant or *(here)* annoying way – 13 **to forge** [fɔ:dʒ] *fälschen* – 21 **sap** watery substance in a plant – 22 **to tend** to look after – 25 **to jabber** to talk quickly – 26 **jackal** ['dʒækəl] dog-like animal that eats dead animals – 26 **to cackle** onomatopoeia *(Lautmalerei)*: can you hear the sound the jackal makes?

Susie laughed, a strange, dry, choked laugh with no sunshine in it. "Today is my wedding day," she said. "Your Uncle Thomas is my husband. Do you understand that, Abela?"

"No," said Abela, trying to pout.

"Neither do I," said Susie. "All I want is to go back home with Thomas, and be happy."

"Happy," said Abela. "I know the word happy."

"Are you happy, Abela?"

"No," Abela said. "No Mama. No happy."

Bibi had made them a wedding feast of beans and chillies cooked with bananas and rice, and a special pudding of mangoes cooked in coconut milk. She was angry when she saw that Thomas wasn't with them.

"Where's he gone?" she asked Abela. "To the pombe, I suppose."

"He's getting the documents," Abela said.

"Tch! Documents!"

They waited till after dark for Thomas to come, and when he didn't come they ate without him, sitting outside around the charcoal fire so the smoke inside the hut wouldn't make Susie cough. The stars were huge and brilliant, the frogs and the insects were singing loudly and brightly.

It was morning when Thomas walked into the compound. He ignored Susie and went straight to his mother.

"I can't get a passport for Abela. She can't leave when Susie does," he told her. He paced round her, kicking angrily at the skinny cat who was mewing round their feet for the coconut milk. "They're idiots, those men. They said they knew someone who could find me one in time."

His mother clicked her tongue. "It is not good to do things this way," she said. "It is not lawful."

"Who cares about the law!"

4 **to pout** to push out your lower lip, for example when sb is unhappy – 31 **lawful** legal

"What's the matter?" Susie asked.

"Nothing," he told her. "Just some hold-up with the travel documents."

"What documents?" Susie asked. "I've got my passport, it's ok. We are properly married, aren't we, Thomas?"

"Hey, I tell you, we're mister and missus now!" He pulled the signed marriage certificate out of the back pocket of his trousers to show her, and another paper fell to the floor. Susie bent to pick it up, and read the words before Thomas had time to snatch it away from her.

"Aids? HIV?" There was a frightened, frozen silence. Susie's face had gone very white. "Aids? What does this mean? Aids? Why have you got these papers?"

"It's just a certificate my mother got for Abela. I'll tell you on the bus, ok?"

But Susie's breath was coming in quick, sharp gasps. She backed away from Thomas. "Are you telling me these people have Aids? And I've been sleeping here? I've been eating and sleeping with people who have Aids?"

"They don't have Aids. These are papers to show they *don't* have Aids." His voice was low and reasoning, pushed out between his teeth, urging her to be calm and quiet. Pimples of sweat were breaking out on his forehead.

"Is that what your sister died of? Aids?" Susie's voice was rising to a pitch of hysteria. "It is, isn't it? Why didn't you tell me? You bring me here, knowing all this?"

Realising that Susie was upset, but not knowing the reason for it, Abela ran to her, wanting to put her arms round her pale princess, but that made Susie panic even more.

"Keep away from me!" She shouted. "Don't touch me. Go away."

It was impossible for Thomas to calm her down. Susie refused to go back into Bibi's house again, convinced that she

2 **hold-up** delay, problem – 10 **to snatch away** to take away abruptly – 16 **to gasp** to breathe suddenly – 21 **reasoning** thinking carefully – 22 **to urge** [ɜːdʒ] to plead *(inständig bitten)* – 22 **pimples** spots in one's face *(Pickel)*

would catch Aids if she touched anything belonging to them. Abela and her grandmother stood together, bewildered and frightened, understanding nothing of what was going on, of the white fury that had taken possession of Susie. In the end Thomas took Susie to the teacher's house, which wasn't a round mud hut like his mother's but a concrete building with four rooms. He asked Mrs Long to explain to Susie that she couldn't catch Aids by sleeping in the house where HIV Aids victims had lived, and to show her the documents that testified that his mother and Abela were clear of the deadly disease. In spite of all Mrs Long's reassurances, Susie was still too upset and afraid to go back to Bibi's house. In the end the teacher said she could stay there with her until the time came for her to leave for the airport at Dar-Es-Salaam.

"She stays with me," Thomas insisted. "She's my wife."

They both stayed at Mrs. Long's that night. In their plain room, an electric fan whirred into the sweaty heat. Susie nervously watched the lizards scurrying across the ceiling. She had had enough. All she wanted now was to go home. Coming to Africa had been a big mistake.

The next morning they left for Dar-Es-Salaam. Bibi and Abela went to the bus station to say goodbye to them; Bibi gave Abela a little basket made of banana leaves to give to Susie. Abela was fretful, keeping her head down, not daring to look at Susie in case she started shouting at her again. When Susie crouched down to smile weakly at her she felt as if the world had started turning again.

"Please don't go home," she said. She had practised the English words all the way to the bus stop.

"You be a good girl. Help your grandma," Susie said. She ferreted in her bag and brought out a little key chain made of

2 **bewildered** [bɪ'wɪldəd] confused – 4 **to take possession** [pə'zeʃən] **of** to control, to have power over – 9 **to testify** to confirm, prove *(bezeugen)* – 10 **to be clear of a disease** [dɪ'zi:z] not to be ill – 11 **reassurance** [ˌri:ə'ʃʊərəns] confirmation – 16 **plain** simple – 24 **fretful** anxious, complaining, unable to relax – 31 **to ferret** *(inf)* to rummage, to search for sth in a panicky way

coloured beads, with a tiny mirror dangling on the end of it. “Here. This is for you, Bella.”

“Look, look Bibi!” Abela gasped. “Look what Susie has given me!”

Her grandmother turned it over in her fist. The little mirror flashed and sparkled, catching winks of blue sky and dithering leaves in its glass.

“Do you like Susie?” Uncle Thomas asked casually.

Abela flung her arms wide open and danced round Susie. “I love her! I love her this much!”

“I'll sort the passport out when I'm in Dar,” Thomas told his mother. “We'll have to send the kid over on her own, then I'll get my own visa sorted out. Meanwhile, get her clean. You know what I mean, mama. And get that teacher to give her extra English lessons. It'll be easier for her that way.”

He climbed on the bus after Susie. Abela ran alongside, waving, and Susie, pale and still upset, full of misgivings, waved back. Only when the bus had completely disappeared from sight, and the roar of its engine had disappeared, would Abela agree to go to school with her grandmother.

“So you like that lady, Uncle Thomas's wife?” Bibi asked as they waited together to speak to Mrs Long.

“Yes,” said Abela. “She's very pretty. I wish she would stay here with us.”

Bibi nodded. Maybe Thomas was right. Maybe it was selfish of her to want to keep Abela in the village without a mother and father. What was there for her here?

“How good is Abela's English?” she asked Mrs Long.

“Very good,” the teacher smiled. “She's a very clever girl. She learns very fast.”

“Does she?” Bibi's heart was big with pride. “Give her lots of English words, Teacha. She's going to live in England with her new mother and father.” She looked down at Abela's startled face. “There,” she said. “Now you know, Abela. Now you have your Uncle Thomas's surprise.”

6 **dithering leaves** *flatternde Blätter* – 17 **misgiving** doubt *(Zweifel)*

Chapter 9

ROSA

I really enjoy writing in the stripy book that Molly gave me. I've told the book lots of things that I've never told anyone else. I've even drawn sketches of me on the skating rink, Mum on the rink, Molly and her shoes. I think it was all avoidance tactics really, because the first and most important thing, the big WHY, has been there at the front of my mind all the time. Maybe I'm scared of what I might find out.

"You're not good enough, Rosa," Mum might say. "I wanted a different kind of daughter." She might. We're not a bit alike, Mum and I. We don't look alike, we don't act alike. But I needed to know, didn't I? I had to.

I waited for the right moment. The trouble is, Mum never stops. So I made the moment happen. I took down the teddy-bear curtains from my bedroom and plonked them on the kitchen table.

"Oh," Mum said, frowning. "Do they need washing?"

"They need throwing," I said. "I don't know if you've noticed, but I'm thirteen and a quarter years old these days."

"Right. Well, I had noticed, because you've suddenly become utterly gorgeous, but I'd stopped noticing the curtains. I'll wash them and take them to Oxfam. Some cute seven year-old will love them."

We started to take the plastic hooks out together, and that was when I took a deep breath and blurted it out.

"Mum. Why do you want to adopt another girl?"

6 **avoidance** [ə'vɔɪdəns] preventing sth bad from happening *(Vermeidung)* – 19 **throwing** *here:* throwing out, getting rid of – 22 **utterly gorgeous** ['gɔːdʒəs] extremely nice, beautiful – 23 **Oxfam** second hand charity shop that raises and donates money to starving people – 26 **to blurt out** to say sth suddenly and without thinking

Then *she* took a deep breath and fiddled with her impossible hair for a second, scooping it back behind her ears. “Not just any other girl, Rosa. I want her to come from Tanzania.”

And that set my head reeling. It just shows, doesn’t it, if you don’t ask, you don’t find out. I might never have known.

“You didn’t tell me.”

“Well, Molly and I agreed that it wasn’t what you needed to know, not at first. You needed to get used to the idea of adopting a sister at first. Of including a new person in the family. That was what we really needed to talk to each other about. But you really didn’t want to. You didn’t want to talk about the idea at all. So Molly and I agreed not to pursue it.”

That’s what she said, and that really was the answer to the question, and it was all I wanted to know at that moment. I needed to go upstairs and think about it. I needed to write it all down in the stripy book. It really did explain everything.

And this is the reason: I’m black. I’m from Tanzania. Although I’m British, I was born in Africa.

And my mum is white.

Later, after tea, after I’d done my homework and had my bath, I came down in my red winter jim-jams and snuggled up to Mum. She was writing a report of some kind, but she put it down straight away and looped her arm round my shoulder.

“So, to answer your question,” Mum said. “Why do I want to adopt another girl? Well, I think it would be wonderful for you to have a Tanzanian sister. I’ve always thought that, though it’s taken me a long time to realise that adoption is the only way that this can happen. I’m never going to live in Tanzania again, much as I love it. This is my home. And I just feel now is the right time.” She pushed her hair behind her ears; I know when she does that it’s because she has important things to say. “It’s not easy to get accepted as an adoptive mother though.”

1 **to fiddle** to touch here and there, *here:* to play – 12 **to pursue** [pə'sju:] *here:* to continue to talk about – 21 **jim-jams** *(inf, abb)* pyjamas

"Have you been accepted?" I asked.

"No."

"Was it because I didn't want to adopt?"

"Yes, Rosa, it was. We had to be accepted as a family."

She went out to the kitchen to make a drink. Long past my bedtime, and she hadn't told me to go up yet. I was nearly ready. I followed her into the kitchen.

"Mum, can you ask Molly to come again?" I said. "I really, really want us to adopt. I really, really do."

Chapter 10

ABELA

It was two months before Abela's passport arrived, and meanwhile she heard nothing from Susie, her white princess, or from Uncle Thomas.

During that time, a cousin came to tell Bibi that Abela's aunties in her old village had died of HIV Aids. Bibi grieved again; all her daughters were dead now.

Women from the clinic came to each household to talk about protection from Aids. It was all more than Abela could understand.

"Will we all die?" she asked Bibi, and the terror of the thought kept her awake at night. Whenever she thought about it she felt as if she was letting go of herself; she felt as if she was spinning in a vast lonely black sky, with no stars, no moon, nothing but blackness. Bibi would hear her struggling to wake herself out of nightmares and would hug Abela close to her, folding her in her arms, rocking her.

"Sssh, baby, sssh. You're quite safe. This country is cursed now, that's what my friends tell me. It's not our faults, we're not bad people. What did we do wrong? We work hard and we pray and we look after each other. And still we get sick, and when we are sick, there's not enough medicine to help us. But when Thomas takes you away from here, I'll be happy for you." She clasped Abela's face in her hands. "I'll have to get you ready, so that when he comes, you can go."

And one day soon after that my Bibi who loves me so much did to me the thing that gave me so much pain that I thought I was

19 **cursed** ['kɜːsd] *verdammt*

going to die. She woke me up early and she said, "Abela, today we have to get you clean. We have to get you ready for when Thomas comes."

She is full of some deep secret, and her face is smiling though her eyes are tight and dark. She says, "You are nine years old, Abela. I can't let you leave this village until you are ready. You'll see. You must be clean before you go."

I am still puzzled, and I am a little afraid now. Then she tells me that she has sent for the medicine woman to come from another village, and then I know as much as I have ever known. I have heard the whispers when girls go away from my school and sometimes don't come back for weeks, and when they come back they walk like old women for a time, as if their bodies and their legs are separate things. And sometimes they don't come back at all. They are never seen again. The hyenas have taken them, the village women say. These are things that I have known all my life, things that I am so afraid of that I can not think about them, can not believe they could happen to me, that my beautiful kind, loving Bibi would do these things to me.

Bibi and her friend come to find me when I am playing with my Coca-cola car in the ditch. They come and call my name and stand with their arms folded, waiting, and I know that my time has come and I am weak and trembling with fear. I want my mother. At first I pretend not to hear them but the air is beating wildly round my head like the wings of angels and I know I have to do what they tell me to do. They take me gently by each arm but I am still clutching my car. They take me down to the red fire tree at the bottom of Bibi's field, and there the old medicine woman is waiting.

She has a knife and she is sharpening it on a stone. I have to lie down on the earth and Bibi puts her hand over my mouth so I won't scream. I look up at her and she is watching me with shame and love and pity and pain and all these thoughts in her eyes seem to go back hundreds and hundreds of years.

The angel wings are beating so fast around me that I have lost myself.

When I wake up I am in Bibi's hut. The pain between my legs where the medicine woman cut me is so sharp that I want to scream, but the screaming is in my head, and the only sound I make is a whimper like the little mew the kittens make. Bibi comes to me and takes my hand and says, "Good girl. Now you are clean, Abela. Now you can be a woman."

It is days before I can walk again, and then I can only hobble, pressing my thighs together. I have been stitched up so tightly where they cut me that I feel the knife pain again every time my water comes between my legs. I think the pain will last forever. I think I will die of it. But by the time Uncle Thomas comes for me, I am healed. Now I am clean. But when was I dirty?

She saw Uncle Thomas coming from the bus, but because he was on his own this time she didn't run to him. She squatted down with the younger children, head bent so he wouldn't see her. She had a toy car made out of a Coca-Cola tin, red and silver. Her father had made it for her years ago, and now all the children had made copies of it and scooted them up and down the narrow runs they had channelled out in the yellow earth. Hers was still the best.

Her grandmother called her to the house and reluctantly she picked up her car and ran home. Her uncle scooped her up and tried to kiss her, but she swung her head away so his lips only touched her ear. He dropped her to the ground and she landed on all fours, like a cat.

"Get her ready," he told his mother. "We're going back on tomorrow's bus. She's flying from Dar tomorrow night."

"Tomorrow!" Bibi wailed. She folded her skinny arms across her chest, rocking herself backwards and forwards. "Not so soon! I'm to lose my little girl so soon?" She clutched out at

9 **to hobble** to walk with difficulty – 10 **thigh** [θaɪ] upper part of the leg *(Oberschenkel)* – 10 **to stitch up** to sew together – 14 **healed** healthy *(geheilt)* – 23 **reluctant** against sb's will

Abela's hand. "Will I see her again? Ever? Will you bring her back home to me?"

"Get her ready," Thomas ordered. "I'll fetch her at six." He strode off to the field that belonged to his mother, and stood with his arms folded, watching the rippling stalks of corn. After a while she joined him.

"Abela is ready for you," Bibi said quietly. "But I want to know some things. And for a change, you can tell me the truth, Thomas. "Where did you get all the money for these papers you needed?"

He shrugged. "Can't you guess?"

"Tell me. True words. Tell me."

Her son squatted down on his knees and scooped up a handful of dry earth. He let it trickle between his fingers. Then he looked up at her. Slowly understanding spread across her face.

"My land! You paid for it with my land?"

"*My* land, Ma, when you're dead. Which you soon will be, by the look of you."

"It belongs to our tribe. You have no right to part with it like this," his mother's voice screeched with shock and anger.

Thomas stood up, scattering the last of the dust over her head. "It's done, Mama. And you better get off it right now. It's not yours any more, not even the corn or the beans that grow on it, not even the dust in your hair." He clapped his hands at her, shooing her off the field like a straying hen.

"And I'm poor for the rest of my life!" she wailed. She turned on him, beating him with her fists till he gripped her wrists tightly above her head. "How am I going to live, Thomas?"

"Abela will send you money."

"Abela?"

"I told you. A rich family will buy her. I give half the money to you, Mama. And Susie is my wife now – she can come and

5 **to ripple** *sich kräuseln* – 5 **stalks** *Stängel*

go as she pleases, and when I get to England, I can help her. We'll find more little girls to take to England, more and more. There's no end of rich homes for them. I'm a good son. I'll give you a share. Soon you'll be able to buy your land back. Now what do you think of my plan? Mama, I'm your clever son, not your bad son. I'm good and kind to my old mother."

After all, there wasn't much more to be done to get Abela ready. Her grandmother had already bought her a new kanga for the wedding, and it had not been worn since. She took some precious last dried beans and eggs down to the market and when she had sold them, she bought Abela a second kanga, blue like the sky of Africa. It had a frieze of letters stamped round it. *Ut anikumbuka.* You will remember me. One of Bibi's friends gave Abela some old sandals to wear; they were too big, and her feet slipped about inside the loose straps.

"You'll need them," she told Abela. "Everybody wears them in Europe."

They had been a present, posted from Amsterdam many years ago by a tourist who had befriended her. Abela's feet slopped from side to side in them as she ran to the schoolhouse to say goodbye to Mrs Long.

"So you're really going," Mrs Long shook her head sadly. "I wish you weren't, Abela. I hope things will be all right for you there. My word, you'll be cold in England!" she pretended to shiver, pretended to laugh. "What clothes are you taking?"

"My kangas and my new shoes," Abela told her, with a touch of pride in her voice.

"Here. You'd better have something warm." Mrs Long went into her bedroom and came out with a red cardigan. She slipped it round Abela's shoulders and smiled. "It's huge on you, but the colour suits you."

10 **precious** ['preʃəs] valuable, worth a lot (usually — but not here — of money)

"Thank you for my something warm," Abela said, hugging it round herself even though it made her feel sticky with its heat. "And thank you for my English words."

"I'll miss you Abela. Never forget how beautiful this country is."

"Yes Teacha. One day I come home. One day I be doctor, I come home, and I make people better." She puffed out her cheeks and giggled. It had been a huge sentence for her to say.

The next morning the whole village turned out to say goodbye to Abela.

"Habari, habari Abela," they called to her, laughing excitedly. "Goodbye, Abela."

She clutched her new kangas and her Coca-Cola car and the mirror key ring rolled up in the red cardigan; she had nothing else to take.

"Be a good girl," Bibi said to her. Her voice was breaking into little pieces.

Suddenly Abela realised the enormity of what was happening. She clung to Bibi, clasping her hands together tight round the old woman's waist, and had to be pulled away roughly by Uncle Thomas as the bus engine revved for departure.

"Tell you something, Abela," he said quietly. "Take a long last look. This is the last time we'll be here. Ever."

He pushed her up the step and she scrambled to a seat by the window, desperate to wave goodbye to her grandmother, to her friends, to all the villagers, to Mrs Long, to the priest who was at that very moment parking his motor bike outside the school; all waved, all smiled, all became ghosts in the shimmer of yellow dust.

8 **to giggle** ['gɪgəl] *kichern*

At last they arrived at the airport. Abela slopped clumsily and tiredly in her loose sandals after her uncle as he hurried her into the frantic airport building.

"Is this Europe?" she asked, and was ignored.

Her uncle fished in his rucksack and brought out a loose headscarf, which he draped around Abela's head, covering most of her face. It made her feel hot and sweaty. She tried to pull it off but he slapped her wrist.

"Keep it on till you see Susie," he ordered her. "It might help." He brought out a pair of loose cotton trousers and told her to step into them. Then he stood back. "That's better," he said. "Now you can be anybody."

He hurried to catch up with two African Asian women who were joining the queue at the check-in desk. His shirt was dark with sweat. Abela swayed beside him, half-asleep, clinging onto her red bundle. The women in the queue offered her a banana and she took it in grateful silence. Now she could hear her uncle shouting at the man at the desk, arguing in his bullying voice, but she was too tired to try to understand what was going on. He turned his head and gestured towards the women, and the man at the desk nodded and shrugged.

At last it seemed to be over. Uncle Thomas turned round and lifted her up. His face was bright with smiles again. "She's happy because she's going to see her mother," he told the women with the bananas, and they smiled at Abela and told her she would be glad of her red cardigan in England. Abela's eyes swam with tears, stinging, tired, uncomprehending tears. How could she be going to see her mother? Her mother was dead.

"The steward at the desk wants to know if there is someone to look after her on the flight," Uncle Thomas told the women.

1 **clumsy** *ungeschickt* – 3 **frantic** very busy, chaotic – 6 **headscarf** piece of cloth that covers the head – 15 **to cling to sth** to hold on tight to sth – 18 **to argue** *here: schimpfen* – 20 **to gesture** ['dʒestʃə] to use your hands and feet to make yourself understood – 21 **to nod** to make a sign with one's head to say yes – 21 **to shrug** to move your shoulders to say "I don't know" – 27 **uncomprehending** not understanding

"All that way on her own!" the older of the two said. "It's a long, long way!"

"My daughter has to travel on her own. Her mother will meet her at Heathrow. I'm coming next week."

"I'll look after her," one of the woman nodded. She smiled at Abela. "Hey, you don't need to cry. You scared of flying? It's fun!"

When the women went forward to the desk to have their documents checked, Uncle Thomas knelt down to Abela and thrust an envelope and a little book into her hand. "This is your passport," he told her. "Never let anyone else have it, right? Cling hold of it all the time. It cost me a lot of money."

So this was the passport, this was what all the fuss was about. She opened it curiously and looked at the shiny picture inside. A little girl stared solemnly out at her.

"That's you," Uncle Thomas said.

She started. "Me? What do you mean, me?"

"That's your picture. Your photograph."

She frowned at it, trying to understand. She knew the word *picture*. She stroked the face gently. Did she really look like that?

"What is this?" she asked, holding out the letter.

"That's your HIV certificate. You're to give that to Susie. She'll be there when you arrive," he told Abela. "Your mummy. Susie. Remember to call her mummy. Always. She's Mummy, and I'm Daddy, not Uncle Thomas any more." His voice was rough, like a dog's, Abela thought. Like a dog that could bite at any minute. "It's very, very important. There could be serious trouble with the police if you get it wrong. I could go to prison. Understand?"

She nodded, but she didn't understand, not a word of it, even though it was spoken very carefully in her own language. She was frightened by the tone of his voice.

"Come on, we've got to get you into the departure lounge." He took her hand and led her to where the two Tanzanian women were waiting for her by the departure gate, and there he squatted down, full of smiles again.

"Give Daddy a big kiss," he said. His hand was hurting her. She let him hug her, turning her face away from him. "I'll be with you and Mummy as soon as I can."

And he walked away quickly, without a backward glance.

I don't remember much about flying to England. It was night when we boarded the plane. It was like getting on a big bus, but I think there were more people on that plane than there are in my village. The two women sat next to me and told me I could have the seat near the window. I didn't think that was a good idea, because it was dark outside anyway, but they just smiled and told me to wait and see. When the plane was setting off I thought it would break up into little pieces; it roared like a herd of charging animals, it rushed like a mighty wind, like the *haboub* of the desert. And then the women told me we were in the air, flying like a huge quiet bird through the night sky; like a massive eagle with people in its belly. I couldn't believe it; even though I had seen these big silver birds in the sky that people called planes, I couldn't believe that I was inside one.

"Look now," one of the women said. She was fat and comfortable and she reminded me a little of Bibi's neighbour. I liked her best.

Out of the window, far below me, I could see millions of golden and silver lights. "The plane-bird's flying over the stars!" I gasped, and she laughed and told me that those lights weren't stars at all, but the cars and house lights and street-lamps of the great town of Dar-Es-Salaam. They were beautiful, like strings of glowing beads. And then the lights were fewer and fewer. We were flying over Tanzania, over the plains and mountains

1 **departure lounge** [laʊndʒ] place where passengers wait before boarding a plane – 17 **herd** *Rudel* – 17 **to charge** to rush forwards in attack – 20 **eagle** [ˈiːgəl] big bird of prey *(Adler)* – 31 **string of beads** *Perlenkette*

and deserts. I thought about Bibi sitting alone outside her little round mud hut, with all the darkness of the night around her. Oh Bibi!

We were flying over Africa, and still I stared out at the huge black empty night. We left Africa behind. Black, black, black, all around the plane-bird. Black.

I woke up hours later, stiff and hungry. The sky was light, and below us were strange deserts curling and cresting and billowing into wonderful shapes, white and golden and pink, and I was told that they weren't deserts but clouds, and the colours were the light of the sun.

I slept again, and I was woken by that terrible charging rush of the herd of animals. It was the plane landing, bumping down the clouds like a bus bumping over rutted roads, and then it was still.

"We've landed!" the Tanzanian ladies said. "You're home!

"Are we in Europe? I asked.

"We're at Heathrow Airport, London, England," the plump one said.

"Europe," added the tall one with the smiling eyes.

"Heathrow Airport, London, England, Europe," I repeated, and kept on repeating while we went through the terminal and waited for their baggage, and all the way through into the arrivals lounge; I held on to it like a chant, because it was a magical song. My village had gone. Tanzania had gone. Africa had gone. Heathrow, London, England, Europe had been put in its place. This was where I lived now.

I looked for Susie among all the white women at the airport. The faces all looked the same, and most of them had yellow hair. White faces, yellow hair, tiny mouths.

At last I saw her, my white princess, my flamingo. She didn't see me; in fact, she walked right past me. I grabbed out at the sleeve of her jacket. And I remembered the right word.

"Mummy!"

She snapped round, frowning, and I remembered then to pull the hot scarf away from my head.

"There you are!"

I put my arms round her waist and hugged her. I could smell flowery perfume on her jacket.

"I thought you weren't coming!" I sobbed in my own language. I couldn't find any English words to tell her how frightened and lonely I felt. *Be a good girl,* my grandmother's voice said to me. *Be strong,* my mother said, in her pretty blue voice. *Be strong, be strong, and be strong.*

I lived with Susie for two months. At first we stayed in a room with a big bed and a box that held all Susie's clothes. The room was as big a Bibi's house, but Susie said it was a dive, which meant it was too small and dark and nasty, and she was ashamed to be living there. "I can't afford anything better. I spent all my money on going to Africa with Thomas," she told me. "And he has every penny that was left. Every damn cent." She lit a cigarette and dragged on it, making her cheeks hollow and ugly. "But I'll get us out of here. You'll see."

One day she wrapped me up in one of her jackets; the sleeves were so long that she had to roll them up, but at least I was warm and snug in it. I loved it because it smelt of her perfume. She took me along to a place called Social Services. She told me to say nothing at all, and I didn't, but I listened to every word, trying to piece the few familiar words together to make some kind of sense, but she spoke too fast, jabber jabber jabber, and all I caught were the words daughter, husband, Africa. Oh, and home. She argued for a long time, while I tried to understand the words that were flying backwards and forwards between them. I hated her angry voice; it made me think of the day she had turned against me at Bibi's house, the day I called the HIV

23 **snug** comfortable – 24 **Social Services** [ˌsəʊʃəlˈsɜːvɪsɪz] *Sozialamt* – 26 **familiar** [fəˈmɪljə] known

Aids day. Then she stood up and walked out, holding my hand tightly. When we were outside she bent down and hugged me, her face bright with a beautiful smile again.

"They've given me a family flat!" she told me, laughing, and I laughed too. I wanted her to be happy like this all the time. "There'll be a bed for me and a bed for you, a little room with a table to cook our meals, and a room all of its own for us to wash ourselves in. And we can have it straight away! All because of you, Abela!"

How I loved it when Susie was happy! She read me stories and made me a book with drawings of animals, and we wrote the names in English and Swahili; Simba, lion. Twigga, giraffe. Kuku, chicken. She drew the pictures and gave me some pencils to colour them in with. On the back page she sellotaped a piece of paper.

"What's that?" I asked.

"It's the paper that Thomas gave you in that envelope," she said. "Keep it safe, Abela. It tells people that you don't have HIV Aids, thank God."

Sometimes she went out to work at a café nearby, and left me to get on with my colouring.

"Can I come with you?" I asked her, but she always refused.

"No. It isn't safe."

"I want to go out. Can I go to school?"

She shook her head.

"When Thomas comes. He said I must keep you at home till he comes. Anyway, you don't need to go to school," she said. "I can teach you." She switched on the television set, the magic box that somebody in one of the other flats had given her. "Watch that. You'll learn everything you need to know."

I don't think she ever switched it off after that. It chattered and screeched all day, coloured lights like eyes blinking, flash,

14 **to sellotape®** to stick with plastic *(Klebeband)*

flash, flash, jangly music, voices, words words words, day and night.

One day she brought me some clothes that someone had given her, and we spent hours sorting through them, cutting them and sewing them so I had a dress and a skirt that fitted me. In those days she was always happy, and I was happy too. She said I made her life better.

And she made my life better. Every time she came home to the empty, flashing chattering flat she brought smiles and hugs and the sharp, cold smell of England with her. Her carrier bag was always full of food from the café – bags of luke-warm chips, soggy apple pie. We ate together in front of the television and she told me funny stories about the customers.

But things changed. Something was wrong, but I didn't know what. Thomas was supposed to be ringing her every week and she would go out to the phone box on the corner. She wouldn't take me with her. I would sit on the windowsill watching her, waiting for her to come back, and when she did she would be looking white and miserable; she would go to her room and shut the door and stay there for hours. She grew tired of me, and there was nothing I could do to please her.

But the worst thing was the fact that she wouldn't let me go out. In all that time, two or three months or more, I only went outside twice, once to the Social Services and once when we moved from one flat to another. I used to sit by the window in my room and look outside at the grey streets and the cars and the restless people. I saw children playing, and wished I could be with them. Even when it rained, I wished I could be outside. But in my country the rain is alive. The rain sings with life. Here it is a grey mist that closes up the world.

One day when she came back from the phone box she was in a different kind of mood. I heard the front door slamming when she came in, I heard her footsteps ringing round the

12 **soggy** soft, watery, *here:* tasteless – 19 **miserable** depressed

stairwell as she stamped up the concrete stairs. She flung open the door to the flat and glared down at me. I was truly afraid. She grabbed me with both hands and shook my shoulders.

"Still not coming!" she shouted. "What kind of a marriage is this? Eh? You knew all along, you brat!" She knelt down, hissing in my ear. "He wants me to sell you to a rich family so he can buy his way over. What would happen to you then, eh? You can thank your stars he isn't coming yet, because that's where you'd be now, Cinderella in the cellar, that's who you'd be. Heard of Cinderella?"

I shook my head, numb with fright at this new passion of anger.

"Heard of slaves then? Think it was all over hundreds of years ago? No way, kiddo. No way."

I still had no idea what she was talking about. Being sold to a rich family didn't sound such a bad idea to me.

"So till he comes and finds somewhere for me, you can be *my* slave! Why not? Pay for your keep for a change."

My eyes were filling up with tears. What more could I do for her? Every day I washed Susie's clothes and put them away nice and tidy. I cooked her lovely food and washed up the dishes and kept the flat clean and sweet.

"There's plenty for you to do," Susie snapped at me. "I've got myself another job at the café – they've asked me to do a bit of washing for them – table-cloths and tea-towels and that. No way, I said. I'm a waitress, me! But you could do that, Bella. And if you don't do it right, I've got a big slap on the end of my arm. Do it right and we'll be friends. Do it wrong and I'll sell you on to someone else. And that would be like sending you to Hell. Heard of Hell, have you?"

"Will I go to the café then?" I asked. That wouldn't be too bad. I would smell the fresh air, I would run, run and feel free.

5 **brat** *(inf)* bad child – 9 **Cinderella** *Aschenputtel*

Susie put her face close to mine. I could smell the sharp, nasty tang of her cigarettes on her breath, and I tried to back away, but she gripped me by the shoulders. Her fingers were like the talons of big birds, like the vultures.

"Come to the café?" she laughed, but it wasn't the white-moon laugh that she used to have. "You've got to be joking. You're not moving from this place till Thomas gets here and sells you on, so you can forget that. You stay here, right here, or you'll go to a much worse place. And don't go peering out of that window either. You've no time for that. Soon as I get the stuff from work, you can get busy. And you can start now." She marched me into her room and pulled out a pile of dirty underclothes from under her bed. "Here you are. Get working on that lot."

Abela could never judge Susie's moods after that. Sometimes she was bewitchingly happy. She would put a CD on and swirl round the flat in her creamy silky nightclothes, a cigarette in one hand with a blush of lipstick on the stub. She would grab Abela by the other hand and make her dance with her, round and round, heads flung back, till they were both laughing and dizzy. Sometimes she would scoop Abela up in her arms and shower her with kisses, and tell her that Uncle Thomas was coming soon, very soon, and she wouldn't let him sell her, she loved Abela too much. They would all live as one happy family.

And at other times she was deep in a black mood, sultry and dark as a cloud of thunder. She wouldn't speak, wouldn't eat the food Abela cooked for her, would sit in front of the television in a deep blue fog of cigarette smoke. At these times Abela would creep quietly about her work, washing the pieces of laundry that Susie brought from the café, hanging them over the radiators to dry, ironing them smooth and crisp, till her back ached and her arms hurt and she longed to lie down and sleep.

2 **nasty** ['nɑːsti] bad – 4 **talon** ['tælən] *Kralle* – 4 **vulture** ['vʌltʃə] bird of prey *(Geier)* – 16 **bewitchingly** extremely, magically – 18 **stub** cigarette end – 25 **sultry** *here:* moody, heavy, threatening

Maybe life is all like this in England, she thought. Maybe this is what all the children have to do. But then from time to time she would hear the high voices of children running to school or playing in the street outside. Only when Susie was out would she dare to steal a glimpse of them from the window.

We never had visitors, ever. Susie had no friends. Then one day there was a knock at the door of the flat. A lady in a very wet blue coat and hair like white feathers showed Susie her identity card and said she was from the social services. Susie tried to close the door in her face, but the lady stepped forward and said she needed to see me, and Susie came into my room and pulled me out, slamming my door behind me. She dug her fingers into my arm, just like Uncle Thomas used to do.

"Keep your mouth shut!" she warned me, hissing in my ear like a fat snake.

The woman sat down and smiled at me. Wet drips trickled down her coat onto the floor. She asked me how old I was, but I was too frightened to tell her.

"She's not very big. You're about seven, I would think."

I knew that was wrong but I daren't say anything.

"We're concerned because you haven't registered your daughter for school here yet," the woman said to Susie.

School! I heard the word and nursed it like a present. How I wanted to go to school!

Susie sat down slowly at the table. I could see that her hand was shaking. She had a red flush across her neck.

"She doesn't speak English well enough."

The woman frowned. "Why doesn't she speak English? Don't you talk to her in English?"

"She's spent all her life in Tanzania. She's been living with her father and her grandmother. Now she's come home." Susie looked at me and smiled, a smile that was as cold as the

21 **concerned** [kənsɜːnd] worried – 23 **to nurse** to look after sb after sb has been ill

window feels when the rain is beating against the other side, and the smile said, *keep quiet.* And I did keep quiet.

"We have been told that you go out to work," the woman said. "Is this true?"

"Sometimes," Susie said. Her voice was shaking. "Just a bit, now and then."

"And do you take your daughter with you?"

"Oh yes."

The woman asked me some questions, and I was too frightened to hear what she said, never mind to answer her. But my head was spinning.

"She must come to school," the woman said. "It's against the law to keep a child away from school, you must know that. She'll soon learn English there."

I wanted to shout then that I could speak English, that Mrs Long said I was the best pupil she had ever taught and that I was clever enough to be a doctor one day: that I wanted, wanted, wanted to go to school. But I stared at the little puddle on the floor and kept quiet.

As soon as the woman went, I asked Susie why I couldn't go to school.

"Because you can't!" she snapped. *Can't* hung in the air like a piece of old rag in the wind. "Not till Thomas comes. I've told you! I can't register you anywhere. We need more papers! Birth certificate, things like that! Why doesn't he send them? Why the hell doesn't he come? Oh, he's got me in such a mess. It's not your fault. It's him. I don't want to be mixed up in his game." She ran her fingers through her hair, and I realised then how limp and ragged it looked these days, not at all golden and glowing like it used to be. Her face was thin and she had dark caves round her eyes. For a moment she softened; for a moment she put her arms round me and held me tight. "I don't know what to do!" she said, in a wailing voice like a little girl,

18 **puddle** *Pfütze* – 29 **limp and ragged** ['rægɪd] hanging down in an untidy and unattractive way

but when I lifted my arms up round her waist to comfort her, she pushed me away.

"Why did you have to come!" she hissed. "Everything's gone wrong! I don't want you here!"

I longed for home. I spent hours in my little room, gazing out of the window at the forbidden street outside. I longed to be running barefoot from my grandmother's house to my school, or playing in the sand with my friends, or singing in the church with the birds swooping in and out and right through because they thought it belonged to them. Bibi, Bibi, I used to whisper, so my breath made a little cloud on the glass. And sometimes in the night I would hear Susie whisper, "Thomas, Thomas." I knew then that we were whispering about the same thing. I would never see Bibi again, I knew that now. And Susie knew that she would never see Thomas.

The lady came back, several times, but Susie didn't answer the door. She called through the letterbox to us, and Susie kept her fingers pressed into my arm, so they hurt. Her long talon nails cut little circles into my flesh. When the woman went, silence swirled round the flat like a cold mist.

"Perhaps I should go to school," I said at last.

"Oh go then, go!" she snapped. "Go to Timbuktu, for all I care!"

But she didn't take me to school, and I had no idea where to go. So, one day, I decided to just find it. I took my chance on the morning she stayed in bed instead of going out to work. She said she had a headache, and didn't want to eat the breakfast I made for her. There was the key, on the table next to her bed. There was my freedom. I put her cup of tea down and slid my fingers round the key.

"Go away," she groaned. "Just leave me alone."

My time had come to be strong. I decided not to wear the clothes that Susie had made for me, but to wear the clothes from home, so I would feel proud and brave. I put on my favourite kanga that was as blue as the sky of Africa, and Mrs Long's cardigan, and the shoes that Bibi's friend had given to me. I let myself out of the flat with the key, and I tiptoed down the echoey concrete stairs.

It was bitterly cold. The sharp wind knifed between the blocks of flats. White flakes drifted on it. Abela thought they were flakes of ash from a fire somewhere, but when they settled on her they melted and gleamed into drops of rain. She looked up at the fluttering sleet and thought the grey sky was breaking into tiny pieces all round her. She had never been so cold in her life, but she began to run, swinging her arms backwards and forwards across her chest, her loose sandals slapping the pavement. She ran to the end of the street where she had watched children walking with their mothers, and down another, and swung into another. From somewhere nearby she could hear the high, excited voices of children playing; the dream sound. She darted over a road, right in the path of a car that screamed to a halt, and she skipped away from it and down another street, and there, at the end, was a yard full of children. She found a gate and ran into the yard, clasping her hands to her mouth in sheer joy, her face so full of smiling that it ached.

The children were just beginning to file into the school building. Abela followed them in. Some of them turned their heads to stare at her, and exchanged smiling looks at the strange way she was dressed on such a cold morning, but apart from that nobody seemed to take much notice of her. The children made their way to a large hall and sat cross-legged on the floor, and so did she. Now she was noticed. A man wearing

9 **to drift** *here:* to fly – 12 **to flutter** to move one's wings – 12 **sleet** half frozen rain – 16 **pavement** path at the side of the road for people to walk on – 20 **to dart** to run quickly – 21 **to skip** to jump

a brown woolly jumper leaned forward and tried to catch her attention, but then, another man walked up to the front of the hall and turned to face them all, and the hall went completely silent.

"Good morning children," the new man, the school head teacher, said.

A chorus of children's voices rumbled "Good morning Mister Helliwell. Good morning everybody."

"Good mornin' Teacha!" Abela called out, and some of the children in the row in front of her turned round to stare. She grinned back at them. The head teacher talked on and on, and Abela gazed round the hall at the bright pictures on the walls, the high windows with their long, colourful curtains, the shiny black piano, the line of teachers sitting on chairs along the side of the room. The man with the brown woolly jumper was staring intently at her again. He was nice, she thought. She smiled at him, and he wiggled one of his fingers at her. She didn't know it was a signal for her to go to him, so she lifted her hand and did the same, then laughed and covered her face, rocking herself backwards and forwards out of sheer happiness.

There was a sudden scuffling sound, and she realised that the head teacher had stopped talking and all the children were standing and turning to face her.

"Jambo!" she said.

The children immediately facing her giggled.

"Turn round!" one of the girls whispered. "Go to class!"

But the teacher in the woolly jumper had moved forward now. He told his children to go to class and sit quietly and wait for him, then he touched Abela's arm lightly and led her away from them. He stopped near the headmaster, folded his arms and smiled at Abela. She smiled back.

16 **intently** giving careful attention – 22 **to scuff** *schlurfen*

"Now then. Who are you?" he asked, too quickly for her to understand.

She frowned. "Mornin' Teacha," she tried.

"Ok. I'll try again. What is your name?"

"Oh. My name is Abela."

"Bella?"

"I am called Abela Mbisi. How are you?" Mrs Long had taught her to say that. Far, far away, in another life.

"Hello Abela," he said slowly. "My name is Mister Hardy. Come and meet Mister Helliwell."

He took her over to the headmaster and said, "This is Abela Mbisi, and I've never seen her before. Is she one of ours?"

"Bella Mbisi," the head teacher repeated. "No, I don't know that name. Come with me, Bella, and we'll sort you out."

She followed Mister Helliwell. She was frightened in case he was going to take her back to Susie's flat and leave her there, but instead he led her into a room that was full of books and papers, photographs of groups of beaming children, and gleaming trophies. A woman sitting at a desk near the window looked up and smiled at her.

"Hello!" she said. "What a lovely dress."

Mister Helliwell sat down on a green leather chair that swivelled from one side to another, and pulled some papers towards him. He looked at Abela thoughtfully, then took a pen from a jar and clicked down the nib. He handed the pen to Abela.

"Can you write your name?" he asked.

She wrote slowly and carefully, anxious to show him how good her handwriting was.

"Ah. *Abela.* I see. Now Abela, where do you live?"

She frowned. She had no idea.

"Do you understand?"

3 **to frown** *die Stirn runzeln* – 18 **beaming** *here:* happy – 23 **to swivel** to move back and forth – 25 **jar** glass container

"Yes Teacha." She brightened up, remembering her chant. "Heathrow airport, London, England, Europe."

Both Mister Helliwell and his secretary smiled. "Ok. That's very good. And where do you sleep?" he asked.

"In my bed." She was very pleased with her English. She thought that must be why he was smiling.

"Where's your mother?" the secretary tried.

"Mama is dead."

Mister Helliwell bowed his head for a moment. "Your father?"

"Baba is dead."

"I see. And who brought you here this morning, Abela? Do you understand? Who looks after you? Where do you live? Who do you live with?"

Oh dear. So many questions. All Abela wanted was to show him how good she was at English so he would let her stay in school. "I live in Africa," she said slowly. "But now I live in Susie house."

"Where is it, Abela? What's the address?"

She didn't know that word, address. She closed her eyes, trying to picture the flat and the view from the window. Where was it? It was in a street. "Social Service house," she said at last.

"Good girl," said the secretary. "That's a big help. I'll see what I can find out."

"Could you take me there?" Mister Helliwell asked.

She drew away, biting her lip. The thought of being taken back to the flat was more than she could bear, to be locked up again day after day, week after week, till Uncle Thomas came. "Please Teacha, don't take me back. I want stay here." There was something like a hard stone in her throat, so hard that she couldn't swallow. She could hardly speak. There was more to say, she knew that, before the stone could be dislodged. But if she said what she wanted to say, it might bring terrible trouble. She put her hands over her face, and Mister Helliwell's

9 **to bow** [baʊ] to lower – 31 **to dislodge** to take away

secretary came and knelt by her and put her arm across her shoulders.

"It's all right, Abela," she whispered. "You can tell us everything."

Abela took a deep breath. "Susie not Mummy," she whispered back. "She pretend so we get social service flat." The secretary nodded, encouraging her to say more. "She say me I not come to school. No papers, no birth tifick."

"No Birth Certificate. I see. What about a passport?"

"Susie tell me it pretend passport, it bring very bad trouble."

There, it was out. She saw the slow look that Mister Helliwell exchanged with his secretary. She heard his deep, deep sigh.

"Illegal immigrant," the secretary said.

"Looks like it. Looks very like it," Mister Helliwell agreed." Oh dear."

Abela lifted her head, deeply scared now. She had one last chance, she felt, before he sent her to prison. "But I want come to school. I want be clever doctor. All people sick, all people dying, like Mama, like Baba. Like my baby sister." Now the tears were pricking her eyes, but she forced them back. *Be strong, be strong, my little kuku.*

"Look Abela, I'll tell you what we'll do," Mister Helliwell said. "You can stay in Mister Hardy's class this morning while I sort out what to do with you."

Mister Helliwell led her to one of the classrooms and tapped on the door. She twisted the corner of her kanga into a tight knot in her fist when he pushed open the door and all the children turned round to stare at her.

"I think Abela would like to make a nice friend here," he said.

Mister Hardy smiled at her. "Welcome, Abela," he said. "How about sitting next to Jasmine?"

21 **tears were pricking her eyes** she was starting to cry

A girl with olive skin and gleaming black hair patted the empty seat next to her, and there she sat, quiet and wide-eyed, watching Mister Hardy as he walked about the room, soaking up the atmosphere of the classroom, and whenever anyone looked at her she smiled for utter glee. She was in school at last.

At lunchtime she joined the jostling queue in the school hall with Jasmine for something called cheesy squares and cabbage, served on a yellow plastic plate. She chose a banana as well, because she hadn't seen one since she left home. She and Jasmine ate side by side, saying nothing, giggling from time to time. She felt perfectly happy, until somebody came and told her to go to Mister Helliwell's office. Her happiness drained away from her. So, she thought, he has found out what to do with me. Maybe he will whip me now because I have no papers.

As she stood outside the office she could hear a familiar voice, and she shrank back, trying to remember where she had heard the voice before. She associated it with Susie's red anger moods, and it frightened her. She turned to run away, but Mister Helliwell came to the door and nodded to her to come in. There was a white-haired stranger sitting there, and Abela recognised her at once as the woman who had come to Susie's flat and told her that Abela should be at school.

She smiled when she saw Abela, and held out her hand to her. "So, Abela, you found your way to school after all. I'm very pleased. Do you like it?"

Abela nodded. "Please no go home."

"Don't worry. You can stay here today, and you can come back tomorrow."

5 **glee** extreme happiness – 7 **to jostle** ['dʒɒsəl] to push against someone in a crowd – 9 **cabbage** ['kæbɪdʒ] *Kohl* – 14 **to drain away** *here:* to go away; to leave – 15 **to whip** to beat – 19 **to associate** [ə'səʊsieɪt] to connect – 23 **to recognise sb** to see sb and know who they are

Abela relaxed. The woman stood up and came towards her, then bent down to be close to her. Abela could smell fried tomatoes on her breath.

"Actually, you can't go home tonight, Abela. Not to the flat."

Abela tried to make sense of the words. "Not Susie house? Where is Susie?"

"I'm afraid Susie has been taken away by the police. She has a lot of questions to answer. Do you understand?"

Abela nodded again, but her mind was blank with terror now. All she really understood was the word *police*. This was what Uncle Thomas had warned her about, in his growling dog voice. What had she done? Was this all her fault, after all? Why had she told Mister Helliwell so much?

The woman with feathery hair smiled at her again, trying to show her that everything would be all right. "I'm called Mrs Sanderson. I'm here to help you. I'm going to be your social worker while you're in England. Your friend. And I've already found somewhere for you to live, very near here. Someone who will look after you till you go home to Tanzania again. You have a false passport, Abela. You can't stay in this country. We're going to try to find your family so we can send you home again."

Abela stared at her. There was too much to understand, so she understood nothing. "Where is Susie?" she asked again. She had the corner of her kanga screwed up in both her hands. Gently, Mrs Sanderson eased her fingers open and smoothed the fabric down again,

"Susie's been evicted from the flat. She can't live there any more. She's with the police at the moment." Mrs Sanderson said. She sighed and stood up, tucking a green fabric briefcase under her arm. "You don't understand, do you? She'll be all right, Abela. Don't worry about her."

9 **blank** empty – 9 **terror** fear – 25 **screwed up** turned into a small ball – 27 **fabric** ['fæbrɪk] cloth – 28 **to evict** [ɪ'vɪkt] to make sb leave a house for ever

"Why don't you go back and play with Jasmine," Mister Helliwell said, and Abela turned immediately and ran from his office. Words that made no sense to her buzzed like flies in her head. All she knew was that Susie was in trouble, and that it must be her fault. And was there something about Tanzania? Was she going back tonight? And what about Uncle Thomas? He would be angry, very angry. He would beat her, she was quite sure of that.

Mrs Sanderson stood in the doorway of the headmaster's office, watching her. "Poor child, what a mess. I've been authorised to find a temporary place of safety for her, so she'll be properly looked after in a foster home while she's in this country. She'll be alright now. She'll be back home soon with her own family. And meanwhile, we've found just the right place for her to stay."

10 **mess** *here:* bad, complicated situation – 11 **to authorise** ['ɔ:θəraɪz] to allow – 11 **temporary** ['tempərəri] **place of safety** *vorübergehend sicherer Ort* – 12 **foster home** home with adults who are not your natural parents (foster parents = *Pflegeeltern*)

Chapter 11

ROSA

So Molly came back to see us. It was like Christmas all over again, I was so excited. I half expected her to bring my new sister with her, but she came on her own, with forms to fill and lots of questions to ask. She asked me if I was really sure about it this time, and I said, yes, yes, a hundred per cent yes, as soon as possible.

She came again a few days later and met Nana and Grandpa, who said they fully supported Mum and me in our decision to adopt, and that they would help us in every way.

And then, we just had to wait. It was all I could think about. Every day I expected to come home and find the new sister sitting there grinning at me in the kitchen; even though Mum and Molly both warned me that it could take months to find the right child, I still hoped. I decided she would be with us by Easter. I would make her a chocolate cake with a little yellow chicken on top. I would share my Easter eggs with her.

Then one day when I came out of school, Mum was there waiting for me, shivering and smiling in the cold March wind. She said that Molly had rung her to say that she was coming round later with some news. My heart dropped right into my stomach. We practically ran home, clutching hands. I went straight up to my room and started to unravel the mess in it. I even took the Dyson up and sucked Twitchy hairs off the carpet. Finally, finally. I heard the car, and I shoved the last lot of socks and books and stuff under my bed. I prettied up the pile of softies and ran to the window, peering through the new mermaid-green curtains.

She was on her own. I was desolate.

25 **Dyson** bagless vacuum cleaner – 28 **softies** *(sl)* bedcovers – 29 **mermaid-green** the same green as a mermaid's tail – 30 **desolate** ['desələt] sad, lonely

When Molly had gone, I ran downstairs again. She had left an envelope on the table with some photographs in, and I knew exactly what they were. They were photographs of my new sister.

"It's not what you expect," Mum warned me. "Molly told me it's hard to find Tanzanian children up for adoption in this country."

I hardly heard her. I opened the envelope, spread out the photographs one by one on the table and stared at them.

They were all wrong. The child was about four years old. It was a boy.

Chapter 12

ABELA

That afternoon, when school was finished, the lady with hair like white feathers arrived, full of bustle and smiles, and took me in her car to a strange house.

"This is where you're going till live, till you go back home," she said. "Come in and meet your foster mother. Her name is Mrs Oladipo, and she's from Nigeria. She has two big children of her own, and two more foster girls, Cathy and Lola. They're both older than you."

I kept my fingers screwed up inside my hands. I could not find words to talk, or mouth to smile. I did not like the house. I did not like the floors that were covered in a kind of red grass. I did not like the big children who gaped and laughed at me there. And I did not like the fat woman who was called my foster mother and who said I must call her Carmel. She did not speak my language. She was loud; she snorted through her nose like a horse. She spat when she talked, shouting at me to make me understand her, shrieking loud laughter when I didn't. I did not like her at all.

And I did not like the man who was called Dad by some children and The Dad by others. He had huge, flat hands which he slapped the table with when he was sitting down, as if he was beating a rhythm on a drum. His face was shiny, his hair and his beard were crozzly white, and his eyes stared at me as if they would make holes right through me. He never smiled, not once, and his voice growled from somewhere deep in his stomach.

14 **to gape** to look in surprise – 19 **to shriek** [ʃri:k] to make a high, loud, screaming sound – 25 **crozzly** (invented word) grey, fuzzy

Carmel showed me up to the room I was to share with the other girls. I had to climb a ladder to get into my bed, and there I found a plastic carrier bag with my other kanga in it, the dress Susie had made for me before she stopped liking me, the book of animals that we had made together, my Coca-Cola car, my pretty key-ring. My passport had gone. I sat on the bed, clutching my car. Carmel wanted me to go downstairs and eat but I wouldn't. She brought me a plate of bread and jam and shouted at me to climb down off my bed and eat it. She was smiling and laughing in her loud, snorting way, but she still shouted, and I covered my ears with my hands and told her to go away.

"Oh, so you're a naughty little girl," she said. "We don't have naughty little girls here. Oh no."

She took the sandwiches away and closed the door. I lay clutching my book and my car while darkness crept around me. The other children came up, and the big girl sleeping in the bed below bounced up and down to make the whole frame shake, and then pushed my mattress up and down from below to try to make me roll off. I didn't care about her. She was annoying, like the grabbing monkeys at home, but I didn't care. I wanted to know where Susie was. I wanted to know what was going to happen to me.

After a bit Carmel opened the door again with my plate of sandwiches in her hand. The other girls lay as still as snakes. She shook my nightie in front of me, laughing and snorting and spraying into my face. I didn't like her. I didn't want to be in her house. She sent me to the bathroom, and when I came back, the big girls were eating my sandwiches. I lay in the dark, listening to them giggling and whispering, and I tried to close my ears till I was in the church at home with the birds swooping in and out and all the people singing in harmony, and Mamma's sweet blue voice rising right up to heaven. But

13 **naughty** *opp of*: good – 21 **to annoy** to anger – 26 **nightie** [ˈnaɪti] *(abb, inf)* night dress

just as I was drifting off to sleep the girl below lifted up the springs under my mattress with her feet, kicking and laughing so I had to cling onto the side of the bed. I wouldn't let myself go to sleep after that. I was frightened that if I did, I would fall into a deep black hole, and I would never be able to climb out again.

I whispered to Susie that I was sorry. *I am sorry. I am sorry.* One of the other big girls shouted at me to shut up but I kept on and on repeating it *I am sorry, I am sorry*. If I stopped saying it, if I stopped hearing my own voice, I would disappear forever into the black hole. The girl got out of bed and climbed up my ladder and started hitting me.

Blue fireflies zizzed in the darkness. Little frogs crickled. Mama sang to me.

13 **to crickle** *(onomatopoeia)* the noise frogs make: to croak

Chapter 13

ROSA

I didn't want Anthony to come. I had set my heart on having a sister, someone nearly my age; a best friend. I could do her hair, I could lend her my clothes. I'd look after her, and share my secrets and my favourite CD's. I didn't want a little boy. But I knew I couldn't let Mum down again. I couldn't change my mind, not this time.

"It's not a girl, Mum," was all I said. "Don't you mind?"

"Well, maybe we have to take what comes." Mum gathered up the photographs like a pack of cards and fanned them out in her hand, selecting one and then another. "After all, a natural mother can't choose whether she has a boy or a girl. And look at him, Rosa. He's beautiful."

He was. He had huge melting brown eyes and a smile that was as wide as a letterbox. Molly brought us a video of him playing with a puppy in his foster-mother's house and he was like a puppy himself, tumbling and play-scrapping and making happy little yapping noises.

After six weeks of occasional visits and two sleepover weekends, Anthony moved in with his little brown suitcase, patchworked with stickers of teddy bears and dogs. For the time being he had the spare bed in my room, the one we'd bought for my new sister. Mum read him stories at night, and he sat with his thumb in his mouth and his eyes going glazy till he dropped off to sleep in her lap. She took two months' adoption leave off work and spent the time clearing out the spidery little spare bedroom. Then she steamed off the wallpaper, singing every minute of the way, and took Anthony on a special trip to

12 **to select** to choose – 17 **puppy** small, baby dog – 25 **glazy** not showing any expression – 27 **spidery** ['spaɪdəri] full of spiders *(Spinnen)*

town and let him choose his own wallpaper. He chose Wallace and Gromit.

Grandpa adored him. He decided to come to the ice rink with Mum and me on Saturdays just so he and Anthony could learn to skate together. Anthony had no fear; within minutes he was out in the centre of the rink, tripping over his own skates, his legs scissoring and splaying, and he didn't care. By the end of the first session he was skating, really skating, a little brown blob with flashing feet, while Grandpa groped his way round the rink bar, clinging on for dear life. The new word for him is *stoical.*

It has to be said that everybody loved Anthony. The postwoman, the window-cleaner, the woman next door, everyone. And if everyone loved him, what was wrong with me? I tried to make him cry, and it didn't work. I nipped him, and he pretended not to notice. I tipped his food away in the kitchen bin and he didn't care. It got worse. My one aim in life was to make Anthony cry.

OK Anthony, I wrote in my diary. I hate your grinning sweety-pie googie-eyed guts.

1 **Wallace** ['wɒlɪs] **and Gromit** ['grɒmɪt] animated characters from UK TV programme of the same name – 3 **to adore** to love – 6 **to trip** to fall – 9 **blob** round mass – 10 **to cling for dear life** to hold on as tightly as you can – 11 **stoical** ['stəʊɪkəl] not showing emotions – 15 **to nip** pinch *(kneifen)* or to bite – 17 **kitchen bin** where the food rubbish goes – 20 **I hate your guts** *(inf)* I hate you very much

Chapter 14

ABELA

Next day, Abela's breakfast remained untouched, but in the morning scramble nobody seemed to notice or to care. Mrs Sanderson arrived when the older children had already tumbled out of the house for their school bus or for work. She brought with her a warm jumper in the same cherry red that the other children in Abela's new school wore, and a grey pleated skirt, black woollen tights and lace-up shoes.

Abela dressed silently in her new clothes, hid her car and book under her pillow, and left the house with Mrs Sanderson, clopping along the pavement next to her in the stiff lace-up shoes that were heavier than her feet. *As long as I can still go to school,* she thought, *it will be all right.*

Jasmine skipped over to Abela as soon as she came through the gate, and they went into assembly together holding hands. *Today I am one of these children,* Abela thought, looking down proudly at her red and grey uniform. *Now I belong.* Nobody stared at her, nobody giggled. In class, Mister Hardy crouched by her table and asked her to read to him from a book with many words, which she did, slowly and bravely.

"That's very good," he told her. "You've been taught very well, Abela."

"Soon I be doctor," she told him. "Go home, make people better."

"Home to Tanzania. I've never been to your country," he told her. "Draw me a picture to show me what it's like."

Abela thought for a long time before she took up any of the coloured pencils. She thought about her village, about

3 **to remain** to stay – 4 **scramble** chaos – 6 **to tumble** to fall – 9 **pleated skirt** *Faltenrock* – 9 **tights** *Strumpfhosen* – 9 **lace-up shoes** *Schnürschuhe*

the dusty red earth were children played and hens scratched, the sun striping through the trees where monkeys screamed and gibbered, the little shembas and paddocks where skinny hump-backed cows lowed moodily to be milked. In the classroom around her, the other children worked at their various tasks, some of them whispering and giggling. She had forgotten about them, or where she was. She was so absorbed in her drawing that Jasmine had to shake her shoulder and take the coloured pencils away from her hand at the end of the afternoon.

"That's a funny house," she said. "It's good though."

When the other children had run out to meet their parents, Abela still sat at her table, not knowing what to do or where to go. Mister Hardy came across and peered over her shoulder at the picture. It showed a round, thatched mud-red hut next to a tree that flamed with crimson flowers. Red and yellow swirls streaked the earth, and the sky was twisting with blue. A huge, yellow sun peered over a pointed mountain, vibrating with light and colour and life.

"This is Bibi's house," she said.

"It's beautiful, Abela." He held the picture up. "Do you know, I can feel the heat throbbing up from the ground! Or is it the sand in the wind? There's so much movement!"

Abela only bobbed her head and laughed. She was so pleased with her picture that she wanted to stroke it.

"And who is Bibi?"

"My grandmother, Teacha," she said softly.

Bibi, oh Bibi. What are you doing now without me? Do you think about me?

All the other children had left by the time Carmel arrived. When they got back to the foster home, Carmel told Abela to run upstairs and change out of her school uniform before tea.

4 **to low** [ləʊ] cows make this deep sound – 4 **moody** unhappy – 15 **thatched** [θætʃt] with a straw roof – 16 **crimson** bright red – 16 **swirl** *here:* large number of flowers – 17 **to streak** a streak is a stripe; the earth was striped – 18 **pointed** having a point at the end *(spitz)* – 22 **to throb** to beat – 24 **to bob** to move your head up and down quickly

In the girls' room she found some different clothes laid out for her on the bed; green trousers and a yellow sweatshirt. Lola and Cathy were in the room changing.

"Take your school clothes off," Cathy said to her." You won't half be in trouble with old Ma Carmel if you don't."

Abela ignored the new clothes, which she disliked, and put on her kanga, Mrs Long's cardigan, and Bibi's friend's sandals. Then she climbed onto her bed to look for her animal book. She wanted to carry on colouring now. Maybe Carmel had some coloured pencils that she could borrow. She could imagine the lion with flashes of black in his golden mane, as if it was lifting as he moved; swirls of air and sand around him. She opened the first page, the simba page, and caught her breath in disbelief. She flicked over page after page. Every one had been scribbled on. The two girls watched her, raising their eyebrows at each other, pressing their hands against their mouths, shoulders shaking with suppressed laughter.

"My book!" Abela gasped, hugging it to her, "My Susie book."

"Her Susie book!" Lola snorted. "Ah! Look, it's all spoiled. What a shame. Who'd have done that?"

Abela dived under her pillow for her car. It was missing. She slid off the bed, losing her balance in her panic, knocking her head on the ladder. The girls smirked at each other as she rummaged under all the beds, searching for the car.

"Where is my car!" she demanded.

"I don't know anything about a car," Lola said. She was twisting Abela's beaded key ring round and round in her fingers, looking at herself in the tiny mirror. "Do you, Cathy?"

"No," grinned Cathy. "Haven't seen anything except that old tin can that fell out of the window."

"Window," repeated Abela. She ran to the window and looked out, and there it was, lying on the pavement below. "My car!" she shouted.

23 **to smirk** to smile in an unpleasant way

One of Carmel's sons was coming down the street. He looked up when he heard Abela's voice, saw the car she was pointing at, and kicked it idly. It clattered into the gutter.

"Oi!" Lola shouted down to him. "Don't leave no litter, ugly chops!"

The boy picked it up and Abela ran downstairs, her loose sandals clapping on the steps, and snatched the car off the boy. She hugged it to herself and refused to part with it, even when Carmel demanded to see it so she could find out what all the fuss was about.

"For goodness sake!" the foster mother shouted. "A battered old pop can! Wants chucking in the bin, that does. Kids, kids, kids. Maybe I've taken on one too many this time!"

Abela didn't see her social worker again until the end of the week. Carmel called her downstairs and said that there was someone to see her, and she ran down eagerly, smoothing her green trousers and yellow sweatshirt, sure that it must be Bibi at last, at last, come all the way from Africa to take her home again. She was bitterly disappointed. She sat bleakly on the settee, head down, saying nothing, while Mrs Sanderson looked through all her notes and drank sweet tea with Carmel.

"How's she been?" the social worker asked.

"Sulky," Carmel replied. "She won't eat her food. But she's quiet enough, not like my other monsters," she laughed. "Like a zoo it is in here these days."

"Are you happy here, Abela?" Mrs Sanderson asked her, when Carmel had gone outside to fetch some washing in. Abela nodded. If she said no, she might be taken away from the school, and she loved every minute of that.

"Where is Susie?" she asked.

3 **idly** lazily, because you have nothing better to do – 12 **to chuck sth in the bin** to throw sth away – 16 **eager** [ˈiːɡə] excited – 20 **settee** [seˈtiː] couch – 23 **sulky** moody *(launisch)*

"Susie's been in prison," Mrs Sanderson told her. "She might have to go back, but she's gone to live with her parents, a long way from here. All right? Understand?"

As long as I can go to school, Abela thought, *I will be all right.*

When she dressed for school again the next morning, Lola and Cathy shrieked with laughter. They didn't even bother to get out of bed. Ignoring them, Abela went down to breakfast.

"Oh, look at this eager beaver," Carmel said to her husband. "Get those school clothes off at once, child. No school today, nor tomorrow neither. Don't know what a weekend is?"

Abela had no idea what to do with herself. Lola and Cathy were allowed to go into town on Saturdays, 'out of my hair," Carmel said, and they piled out of the house full of giggles and high-spirits, reeking of cheap perfume and hair mousse.

"Ah, peace at last!" Carmel said. "Who'd be a foster-mother? Who'd be a mother at all, come to think of it? I must be mad! You can make yourself useful, Abela, if you please. Help me do the beds. And we might go to the shops later. But you can't go out on your own. You're too little. You've got to stay home."

Home. It was true. This was home, this place with red grass on the floor and echoey bedrooms and giggling girls and loud-voiced boys. It seemed it would be home forever.

Every day, every night, she fretted that Uncle Thomas would come and beat her for getting Susie into trouble with the police. Her dreams were so real that she woke up sobbing, and Lola would thump the mattress from the bunk underneath to tell her to shut up.

Thoughts of Uncle Thomas haunted her. The only thing she enjoyed was school, but Mister Hardy noticed that she was often jumpy and frightened, especially if he ever raised his voice in order to speak to the whole class. One day he said, without looking at Abela,

"Children, if you're worried about anything, you know what to do, don't you?"

8 **eager beaver** *here: Streber* – 14 **to reek** *(inf)* to stink – 23 **to fret** to fear, worry – 28 **to haunt** [hɔːnt] to follow sb everywhere – 30 **jumpy** *(inf)* nervous

"Tell the worry box!" the children chanted, hardly looking up from the work they were doing.

For days Abela thought about this worry box, but didn't do anything. But the days crawled and the nights crawled, especially the time she spent at Carmel's house. The only thing she enjoyed was school, but every night Uncle Thomas broke into her dreams, shouting and slapping her with his big, damp hands. One day at break-time when nobody was looking she took a piece of paper and a pencil with her to the toilet. She knelt on the cold tiled floor in the cubicle and wrote "*I am frade of Uncle Thomas. He beat me if you send me home. He want to sell me to rich fambly. I go to hell.* She folded up the letter and walked, trembling, to the worry box. No one was watching. She stood poised with the letter half in and half out of the slot. A door opened and Mr Helliwell came into the hall. She let go of the letter and ran out into the yard, and Jasmine came yelling up to her and grabbed her hands.

That afternoon Mr Hardy whispered to her that she need never worry about Uncle Thomas again. Her social worker came to see her after school and told her that she was very, very pleased that Abela had been able to write the letter to the worry box. Abela felt as if a cool hand was smoothing away the frown between her eyes.

And from then, Abela began to relax, and stopped darting glances at the door or the window every now and again in case Uncle Thomas was there, waiting to punish her. Soon, instead, she replaced the bad dreams at night with good dreams, where Bibi came to see her. In her dreams, Bibi, not Uncle Thomas, was on the plane that rode through the sky. Bibi finds her way to Carmel's house. *Hodi, hodi,* she calls at the door, and Carmel lets her in and says nothing because she has never seen anyone so beautiful and smiling and confident before. Bibi comes into the bedroom and all the taunting and sniggering stops because

10 **to kneel** [ni:l] to go down on one's knees – 23 **frown** *here:* worry – 24 **to dart glances** to look again and again – 26 **to punish** *bestrafen* – 32 **confident** proud of herself – 33 **to taunt** to bully *(ärgern)* – 33 **to snigger** to laugh behind sb's back

she is magical, she has brought the scents of Africa with her. She folds Abela in her arms. "Come back with me now," Bibi says. "It's time to go home." Bibi would come.

"You know lots of English words now, Abela," Mister Hardy told her. "Nearly as many as English children of your age."

"Are there many more words to learn?" she asked anxiously.

"Hundreds and hundreds," he laughed. "Hundreds of words that even I don't know."

The thought of this mystified her. What kind of words could they be that even Mr Hardy didn't know? Where had they come from, and where would she find them? If she knew the names of everything in the world, would that use all the words up? And when all the words were used up, did someone make up more? She fell asleep at night trying to count the number of words she knew.

But too soon, it seemed, she was told that school was to be closed for the Easter holidays.

"Aren't you lucky?" Carmel said to her, spraying her as she laughed. "You've only just got started, and it's the holidays already."

She couldn't bear to think of it. Two weeks without Mister Hardy or Jasmine. Two weeks of shouting Carmel and growling The Dad, of giggling, teasing nights, of listening to Cathy and Lola fighting and crying. Two weeks, she knew, were more than she could bear. She lay in bed watching the moonlight sliding over the rooftops like water, drowning the dark houses with silver light, and she knew what she wanted to do. She was frightened at the thought, but she knew she must do it. *Be strong, my kuku, be strong, be strong.*

She would go home to Bibi.

1 **scent** [sent] pleasant smell – 9 **to mystify** to make sb wonder

Chapter 15

ROSA

It was the day of my level nine when everything went wrong.

I did not want Anthony to come skating with us that day. I asked Mum if he could stay with Nana, just this once. But Mum said that Grandpa wanted to give skating one last chance, so he and Anthony would definitely be coming too.

She didn't understand. I wanted her to say, "All right. Just me and you today, like old times." But she didn't. Those old times had gone forever.

So, I did something stupid. While Mum was in the bathroom putting in her fiddly contact lenses, I got the kitchen scissors and snipped through one of the laces of my skating boots, nipped upstairs with it, and was standing outside the bathroom door wearing a look of total desolation when she came out.

"Look what he's done now!" I wailed, dangling the pink snipped-off lace like a dead worm between my finger and thumb.

Mum simply went in to her room and came back with her rusty Ebay skates, unlaced one of them, and handed the lace to me.

"Use that," she said.

"But it's *black*!" I wailed, I could hear myself, I can hear it now, a silly little-spoilt-brat waily voice, and I couldn't do anything about it. "It'll look awful on my pink boot."

"She could have two black laces," Anthony said helpfully. "That would look better."

"She can have one," said Mum. "And like it."

3 **level** class, grade – 7 **definitely** [ˈdefɪnɪtli] surely – 12 **fiddly** difficult, tricky – 13 **lace** shoelace *(Schnürsenkel)* – 16 **to wail** [weɪl] to cry out – 16 **to dangle** to swing – 24 **spoilt brat** *(inf) verzogenes Kind*

When we arrived at the rink, Grandpa was waiting for us, full of grim determination. Anthony ran to him and flung his arms round Grandpa's legs, nearly toppling him over. Mum said she was going shopping, as she couldn't skate with only one boot.

"I'm sorry Mum," I said, and she gave me a quick hug.

"Good luck," she said. "You'll be fine."

I took a deep breath, *Rise above it*, I told myself, *put it all behind you*. Nana talk, that. I could just hear her. Think about now, go for the *now moment*. That's the sort of thing she says. *Now* is the time that matters. OK Nana. And somehow, it worked. I did everything right. I was a swan. But Mum wasn't there, and I didn't feel any kind of elation. Someone had stolen it away from me.

It was when we were doing the free skating as the public was coming in that the worst thing and the best thing happened. I noticed that Mum had come in. She was sitting near the café with her flask on the table and, I was sure, our muesli bars. I waved to her and began to float, languidly, effortlessly, my very best skating. She would know I had passed, and this was for her, just for her. Then I heard Anthony shouting my name. He was skating towards me, in that knees out, elbow-waving froggy way of his, shouting over the canned music and pointing at my boots. I was furious. He was spoiling my moment for Mum. Did he want everyone to notice my one black lace? Did he want to ruin it all for me, making everyone laugh at me? I turned my back on him.

"Rosa, look at your boots! Look at your lace!"

I ignored him. I stretched one leg behind me and did a slow spin round, just for Mum, building it up, building it up, faster, faster.

"Rosa!" Anthony shouted at the top of his voice. "Look!"

And I did look, and I was too late.

1 **full of grim determination** very determined *(entschlossen)* – 3 **to topple sb over** to push gently, but just strongly enough that they fall over – 11 **swan** [swɒn] *Schwan* – 12 **elation** [ɪˈleɪʃən] joy – 17 **flask** bottle for hot drinks – 18 **to float** *here:* to glide – 18 **languid** [ˈlæŋgwid] slowly – 18 **effortless** using very little energy

One of my laces, the black traitor lace, had come unfastened and had coiled itself round my blade. As I spun, it locked. I lost my balance, crashed over, and a pain like broken glass sliced through my ankle.

People came rushing to lift me up, but Anthony was there first. He was crying. For the first time since I had met him, he was crying. He knelt on the ice, holding my hand in both of his, and the tears were streaming down his cheeks. Two men skated over to me and carried me off the ice, and Mum came running from the café area, white and anxious, and people clustered round, but in all that time Anthony never let go of my hand, never stopped crying. Somebody brought a car to the emergency exit to take me to the accident unit at the Hallamshire hospital, and he ran along beside me as they were carrying me out. I leaned over and hugged him.

"Don't worry Anthony," I said, smoothing his face, wiping his tears away. "I'll be fine."

Anthony and I had a lot of fun together while my ankle was getting better. We did the Lord of the Rings jigsaw that Nana bought for me, and played some crazy computer games. We watched some totally surreal Japanese animations on DVD. I read stories to him, and he and I enjoyed it so much, that closeness, that wonder of story, that I decided to teach him to read. It was the best thing I have ever done, hearing him saying the letters as I pointed them out to him, watching him frown as he tried to make sense of whole words, seeing his face light up as he came to the end of a little sentence and understood it all. Soon he was reading to me, faltering and glancing up at me every now and then to make sure he was getting it right, simple

1 **unfastened** [ʌnˈfɑːsnd] loose – 2 **to coil** to wind around in a series of rings – 2 **blade** sharp metal part at the base of an ice skate – 13 **accident unit** [ˈjuːnɪt] emergency room of a hospital – 14 **Hallamshire** [ˈhæləmʃə] **hospital** [ˈhɒspɪtəl] hospital in Sheffield – 19 **jigsaw** (puzzle) [ˈdʒɪgsɔː] picture cut up into many pieces that have to be put together – 21 **surreal Japanese animations** unrealistic Japanese cartoons – 23 **closeness** contact – 26 **to make sense of sth** to understand sth – 28 **to falter** to stumble *(stolpern)*

words, but he was getting there, and then I would take over and read him some of the wonderful stories that Mum used to read to me.

I love reading, I love words, I hoard them and gloat over them the way I gloat over shoes. I love books. And now I've passed on that love to someone else. Now I know how Grandpa feels when we're playing the piano together, and we make music out of what just looks like a dance of dots and tadpoles on a page. *Richer*, that's how I feel.

Anthony's social worker and Molly came round quite a few times, and it was obvious that they were both really pleased with the way things were going. Then came the big day, nearly three months after Anthony started to live with us, when Molly said,

"Well, Jen and Rosa. You've been having a lovely time with Anthony. Would you like to tell him what you told me earlier? Would you like him to be a member of your family?"

Mum and I dared to look at each other. Her eyes were sparkly, and I should think mine were too. My throat felt as if an apple was stuck in it.

"Yes, please," I said.

"Yes," said Mum. "We would, wouldn't we, Rosa?"

Anthony's social worker said to him, "And how about you, Anthony? Can you remember what you said to me this morning? Would you like Jen to be your new mummy, and Rosa to be your new sister? Would you like to grow up in this family?"

Anthony's eyes were as round as plates. He looked solemnly from one to the other of us, as if he was reaching deep down inside his thoughts to a place where none of us had ever been. I was begging him inside my head, "Say yes, say yes, Anthony." My fists were clenched tight round my knees.

"Yes," he said.

4 **to hoard** to collect – 4 **to gloat** *here:* to feel that they are valuable and to look at them again and again – 8 **tadpole** small creature that grows into a frog or toad – 18 **sparkly** bright – 32 **to have fists clenched tight** *mit geballten Fäusten*

Chapter 16

ABELA

I ran away on Easter Sunday. We had painted eggs for breakfast. Lola had gone to spend the weekend at her cousin's hotel. Carmel went to church, and took her sons and Cathy with her. I would love to go, I would love to sing with all the people like we used to do at home, to listen to the rainbow of sound and slide my own voice into it, my yellow voice. I had not heard my voice singing out loud for months and months. But I knew that this was my chance and I said no, so she shook her head at me and told me to stay in my room and say my prayers instead. The Dad growled at me to say them quietly because he was listening to a cricket match on the radio.

I went upstairs and put my blue kanga on, then wrapped up my poor scribbled-in book and my battered car in my spare one. I left my school uniform and the tights and shoes neatly on my bunk, and I wrote a little note for the secretary. "*Dere Mis Mownt. Thank for the very nice clothe. I hope a notha girl like them too.*"

Then I went. The Dad had fallen asleep over his cricket match; he was snoring like a thundercloud.

I walked out of the house and closed the door softly, so softly, behind me. I was going to Bibi.

15 **battered** damaged

Chapter 17

ROSA

Then things went wrong. Maybe it was Molly's fault, who knows, but it was a terrible, terrible sad thing. What Molly had told us was that Anthony's actual adoption day in County Court would be a mere formality, a signing of papers. Nothing could go wrong now, she promised us. So when her car drew up outside the house one Saturday morning we thought nothing of it. Grandpa was with us, collecting Anthony for his first fishing trip.

Molly came to the door as Anthony and Grandpa were standing there, and her face was full of woe. It told us everything, though she waited till the fishing party had left before she said anything.

"Anthony's father has been in touch with us. I'm afraid, I'm so very, very sorry…"

"He wants him back." Mum's voice was so flat, so empty of colour and shape, that it was like a ghost voice. I hardly heard her.

"But he can't have him back," I shouted full of outrage, full of passionate, hopeless, helpless anger. "He's no right to have him back! Not now."

"He has every right," Molly said sadly. "He's Anthony's father. We could try to fight it, but I'm afraid we wouldn't win. By law, he has every right."

I will never forget that day. I will never forget the day Anthony stood silently by the front door with his little brown suitcase and his fishing rod from Grandpa in his hand. I will never forget

5 **County Court** *Kreisgericht* – 6 **mere** just, only – 12 **woe** [wəʊ] sadness – 21 **passionate** [ˈpæʃənət] showing strong feelings

the knock that told us that his social worker had come for him. But when Mum opened the door, the social worker was sitting in his car and a strange man was standing on the doorstep; Anthony dropped the rod and ran to him and the man bent down and swung him up and they hugged each other as if they would never, ever let each other go.

"Daddy, Daddy," Anthony kept saying. "Daddy, my Daddy."

The man's eyes were closed. His face was wet.

4 **rod** fishing rod *(Angel)*

Chapter 18

ABELA

Just after I left Carmel's house, I saw something wonderful. It was a strange animal, red with a white bushy tail. I don't think anyone else saw him as he sniffed and dipped along the street. He was like a dog, but not a dog. He was like the hyena that howls around the desert places of home, but not a hyena. And when he paused and looked at me with one foot lifted, ready for flight, I went cold and wondering with the thrill of seeing him, and I remembered the lions flickering past me in the night forest. I felt my mother and father standing behind me with their hands on my shoulders, and I felt calm again. Be brave, be brave, their whispers told me, and the red fox slipped away.

I had no idea where to go. I looked up at the sky, squinting at the sharp light of the sun. I could hear the sound of a plane up there, the big silver bird that flew free. Maybe Bibi was on that plane, looking down, full of wonder because now she knew how big the world was. Maybe I should go back to the house and wait for Bibi. But I have waited for Bibi for weeks and months. It is time for me to go to her.

So I started to run, glancing up every now and again to keep the plane in sight so I would know which way to go, but I had not gone very far when a strange man stopped me. He just stepped out in front of me, blocking my way. He had red hair, like the fox, and his face was sharp and thin as if the wind had carved it. He put out his hand to stop me and gripped my shoulder. Then he lifted up my chin and smiled down at me.

"What a pretty girl!" he said.

9 **flight** escape – 9 **thrill** excitement – 10 **to flicker** to shine with a light that goes on and off quickly – 15 **to squint** to narrow one's eyes to see better

I squirmed away. I did not know what to say to him. I was losing my plane; it dipped from sight behind his head. I tried to squirm away but his grip on my shoulder tightened.

"Where are you going to, my pretty maid?" he asked, in a strange, lilting voice like a child singing a song.

But I was ready for that question. I had the answer all ready in my head, the words laid out like a string of bright beads. I had been saying them to myself for many days now. "London, Heathrow Airport, Africa, Tanzania," I chanted. And in my head I added, "Bibi's house," but that was too magic to say aloud. That would be like breaking a spell.

"All that way!" he laughed, cocking his head from side to side. "I hope you've got your passport."

My passport! I had forgotten all about that little book with my shy photograph inside it. It must be still in Susie's flat, in that cupboard underneath the television set where she kept her clutter of things. I broke away from the man and started to run – now at least I knew where I was going, because I had seen Susie's flat many times on my way to the shops with Carmel. Maybe Susie was still there, waiting to take me home.

I could hear the man following me as I ran, calling me to wait because he knew how to help me, and I dodged across the road so a big yellow bus blundered between me and him, and then I darted up a side street towards the flats. I banged on the door, and when nobody answered I kicked it till my feet hurt, and at last the woman from the downstairs flat opened it up. She held a baby in one arm and glared down at me.

"What're you after?"

"Please, Teacha, I want Susie," I said. The baby clenched and unclenched his fist, wrapping his fingers round with the woman's hair.

2 **to dip from sight** to disappear – 3 **to squirm away** to twist one's body to get free – 11 **to break a spell** to stop the magic from working – 12 **to cock** to hold upright – 22 **to dodge** to run quickly, avoiding the traffic – 23 **to blunder** to move in heavily and clumsily – 27 **to glare** to look at sb angrily

"No Susie here," the woman said, uncoiling the baby's fingers. "Gone. Couple of months ago. Didn't you know?"

So it was true. She started to close the door, and I tried to edge inside, to slide like a cat through the gap that she had left.

"No, you don't," she said.

"Please, I want my passport." I could hardly make myself heard over the screaming of the baby; its voice spiralled like knives round the concrete hall and stairs.

"There's nothing of yours there, I tell you. Oh, hang on –" She stepped back and picked an envelope off a pile of letters by the stair. "Is this you – Abela Mbisi?"

She said it wrong, but I knew my name. I reached out and grabbed the blue envelope from her and hugged it to my chest in case she tried to take it back again.

Then she shut the door on me. The screams of the baby still jangled in my ears as I turned away, desolate now, and slumped down onto the step. I put my bundle down and tore open the letter. There was no passport there, just a sheet of blue paper with some scrawled writing on it that I couldn't read. A hand reached out to touch my cheek and I jumped up. It was the man who had followed me before.

"Oh dear, she wasn't very nice, was she?" he said, his voice so drooling with kindness that it made me want to cry.

"I want my passport," I sniffed, trembling to hold back the sobs that were welling up inside me. Be strong, be strong, Abela. Don't cry in front of strangers. I picked up my things and shoved the letter into the middle of the bundle, where it would be safe for me to try to decipher later. I turned away from the man and started to walk down the road.

I had only gone a few steps when the man caught up with me. "London, Heathrow Airport, Africa, Tanzania," he was singing, "Hey ho, a long way to go! Come with me. I can take you to Heathrow airport. I can help you to get that magic thing,

16 **to slump down** to fall down heavily – 23 **to drool** to drip saliva *(Speichel)* (the man's kindness is not real, it is threatening) – 25 **to well up** to rise up — like in a well *(Brunnen)*

you know, that passport? Can't go without that, but I can help you." He held out his hand. His voice was so kind. His mouth was so smiley.

But I looked up into his eyes and saw that he was not smiling inside. How could this be? I did not understand this man, and I did not understand why I was afraid of him. He was giving me hope; my palm trees and my green monkeys, my dusty red earth, my Bibi. If I took his hand, all these things would be mine. But when I looked into his eyes I was more frightened of him than I ever was of the mad mzee swinging her panga to chop off my head in the market place. I was more frightened of him than of the lions who walked by me in the jungle. I backed away from him and turned; I started running, faster, faster than I have ever run in my life. I could hear his feet drumming behind me, his long legs stretched, his long arm reaching out to haul me back. I could hear his voice calling, "Come back child, come back. I'm not a bad man. I want to help you. I want to help you."

I am good at running. I can run fast. I can run for miles and miles and never get tired. I can run in the sweltering heat of Africa. My feet belong to the earth; they are part of it. Long after I heard the man's feet slowing down, long after I heard his voice growing fainter and his breath heaving, long after I couldn't hear him at all, I kept on running. That running was like being free, like turning into a bird, it was like flying. I left everything behind. I left the man with the cruel eyes and the smiling face, I left him so far that I did not know whether he had really been there at all, or whether he was a bad magic dream. I left my happy school and my best friend Jasmine and my special teacher; I left scolding Carmel and The Dad who growled in his belly, and the big girls who hated me. I left it all behind, fear and hope together; I ran and ran until there was nothing left to run away from. When I stopped, I was weak with

20 **sweltering** burning – 30 **to scold** [skəʊld] to angrily criticize sb

hunger and tiredness. I had no idea where I was. I saw a garden with a shed in it, the door swinging open, and I crept inside. I dropped onto my hands and knees, and then I sank onto the wooden floor. I folded up my bundle to make a pillow, and saw again the blue letter with my name written on the envelope. I have never had a letter before. Still lying there, I opened the letter and little by little, I began to untie the tangled sprawl of words.

It wasn't until the next afternoon that Abela was found, in a state of exhaustion. They decided to send her to hospital for observation and there she stayed, deeply asleep between the stiff white sheets of the hospital bed, like the sleeping beauty in the forest. In the locker next to the bed were her clothes, a battered car made out of a Coca-Cola tin, a dog-eared exercise book, and a crumpled blue letter.

When she eventually woke up she found two women sitting on either side of the bed, watching her intently. One was the woman with hair like white feathers. The other was a stranger but not a stranger; a woman out of her dreams with loose hair the colour of lions. I know you, Abela wanted to say, but she was too tired to speak. This woman leaned forward and stroked Abela's hand and spoke to her softly in her own language, the language of hot sun and dry winds, the language of home. Abela opened her eyes again and listened, saying nothing, and it was as if she was listening to a song. Then she drifted back into a calm sleep.

When she woke up again it was a different time of day, maybe a different day. She could hear rain like tiny drumbeats against the window. She closed her eyes again and lay listening to it. It was a sweet sound. Then she focused in on two voices. Some of the words were familiar. Some of them meant nothing at all. She didn't try to understand, just listened to the words.

2 **shed** small wooden building where you keep tools – 7 **to untie the tangled sprawl of words** to decipher (to understand) the words that did not make sense before – 10 **exhaustion** extreme tiredness – 13 **locker** small cupboard that you can usually lock *(abschließen)*

"Maybe we should move her to a different home?"

"I don't think so, not yet. It's not the right time to make changes. And now there's the letter."

Abela opened her eyes at once. She looked wildly around her.

"What is it, Abela?" the woman with lion-hair asked her in Swahili.

"My letter."

"Don't worry. I have the letter. Soon, we'll read it together. When you're better."

Abela stared up at her. She was sure now that she had seen her before. She recognised her smell now, and the way her hair fell softly around her face. She knew her, for sure. She struggled to bring the memory up. It was like a fish, looming slowly and surely out of the murky depths of a river to rise, at last, into light. She had it. "You give me money," she blurted out.

"Money!" Mrs Sanderson said. "Why do you want Miss Carrington to give you money, Abela?"

Abela ignored her. "Miss Carrington," she murmured. It was a nice name.

"What is it?" Miss Carrington spoke to her in her own language.

"You came to my country. You gave me money to make my mother better. You were on the bus."

"Good heavens!" Miss Carrington looked across at Mrs Sanderson. "Would you believe it, Tessie, I know this child already! I met her right at the very beginning of my visit to Tanzania, months ago!" She turned back to Abela. "What happened to your mother?"

"She died," Abela whispered.

Miss Carrington closed eyes and sighed. She remembered the day, of all the days she had spent in East Africa. She remembered the frightened child and her brave, dignified

14 **to loom** to approach slowly and in a threatening way – 15 **murky** dark – 15 **depths** [depθs] *Tiefen* – 33 **dignified** behaving in a calm and serious way

mother. She remembered her feeling of helplessness as she watched the two make their slow, difficult way from the bus to the hospital. Now she was back from her travels, her temporary replacement Tessie Sanderson was handing back her caseload. She had come to the hospital with her that day simply because Tessie Sanderson had told her that Abela was Tanzanian, and it might help her to have someone to speak to her in her own language. She had worked in Arusha some years ago. She knew Swahili well.

Abela at last drifted off to sleep, and Judy Carrington and Tessa Sanderson left together.

"You're not leaving for another month, but I'll take this child on now," Miss Carrington said. "I think she needs some pretty intensive support, and I think it should start straight away."

I do not want to go back to the Carmel lady house, but Miss Carrington tells me she's a good kind lady and I'll be happy there now. I tell her I'm frightened of the big girls.

"They've not been very nice to you," she frowned. "But I'll talk to them, and Mrs Oladipo will talk to them. They're lonely, you see. They've lost their mums and dads too. They've had a bad time."

I say nothing. I stare out of window of her car and I watch the great buses and trucks. When we come to the house Mrs Oladipo gives me a hug, warm and soft like pillows, and Mr Oladipo he growls in his belly and even his mouth turns up and his teeth show to make a smile.

"I've moved your things." Carmel says. "You've got your own room now, Abela. My big lad's got himself a job in Gravesend, so you can have his room for a while. Come and have a look."

I love my new room. It has yellow yellow sunshine walls, and lots of pictures, happy pictures, happy children.

"These are all my children," Mrs Oladipo laughed. "All the children who've stayed in the house with me and Tomi."

4 **replacement** person who does your job while you are away – 4 **caseload** number of people a social worker has to deal with – 28 **lad** *(inf)* boy, son

She bends down and hugs me cuddly soft again, and I never had that hug since I said Bye-bye Bibi. I don't hug back; I keep my arms stiff like trees.

Then she takes me down and I eat my tea and The Dad growls and chuckles and watches TV while I eat, and then he switches it off and goes out to mow the grass and the house is sweet with a green smell that comes through the windows. Miss Carrington comes back from upstairs where she's been talking to Lola and Cathy, and they follow her down and look at me like sheep through their floppy hair.

"Hi Bella, how're yer doing?" Lola says, sloppy with chewing gum.

"Glad you're better, Bella," Cathy says.

I say nothing. I don't look back at them. They go in the kitchen and eat their tea all on their own. Miss Carrington and Mrs Oladipo sit with me on the settee and Miss Carrington opens her bag and brings out my blue letter.

"Have you read this, Abela?" she asks me, and I make my head nod again, but I don't look at her or at anything. I am watching the window where the sound of mowing is coming from but I am not seeing anything.

"I'm going to read it out loud," she says.

I nod again. I bite my lip because I know it will shake. I close my hands tight like knots of rope round my knees. I do not want to hear the words again.

"It's from Susie," Miss Carrington explains to Mrs. Oladipo. "'*Dear Bella, I hope someone sends this to you. I don't know where they've taken you. I have bad news for you. I'm sorry I haven't been a good person to you but I'm not your mother and I shouldn't have pretended I was your mother. I was wrong to do that. Your Uncle Thomas is not coming to England. He is not allowed to come. That is why I married him and why I pretended to be your mum, so he could come here. I think you should go back home now. But I have very bad news for you. Your Uncle*

1 **cuddly** *kuschelig* – 5 **to chuckle** to laugh softly – 10 **floppy** hanging loose – 11 **sloppy** careless – 24 **knots** [nɒts] **of rope** *Seil*

Thomas has told me on the phone that your grandmother has died of malaria. I am very sorry. Love, Susie.'

When Miss Carrington finishes reading the letter in English Mrs Oladipo says, "Oh my God," and holds my hand. Miss Carrington reads the letter in Swahili and I understand some bits better, but the bit at the end I know already, I have understood all those words. I have understood that I will never, never be happy again.

Judith Carrington had to wait until the next case conference was held before she could discuss Abela with her team leader, Denis, and the other members of his team.

Denis glanced down at the notes, reminding himself of the facts. "So she's an immigrant?"

"Possibly illegal, almost certainly an orphan," Judith said.

"And *has* she made progress?"

Judith sighed. She had been a social worker for fifteen years, apart from the year off she had just given herself. In all that time she had seen many children in desperate situations. She never grew hardened to their plight, but she did learn to distance herself. But Abela had touched her in a way that no other child had. "She's been through an awful time. She's had nightmares, cried a lot. I've been visiting her every week for six weeks and now I'm working with Mrs Oladipo to help her through her grief."

"How is she coping with it?"

"She understands that she'll never see her family again. She's let go of that longing. But she needs to have something to put in its place. Hope." She didn't need to utter the word, surely. She was with people who understood how important and how fragile hope was.

"No living relatives?"

19 **plight** [plaɪt] very bad situation – 27 **longing** strong feeling of wanting – 30 **fragile** ['frædʒaɪl] breakable

"She has an uncle. She's very frightened of him. She put a letter in the school worry box to say that he wanted to sell her." Judith riffled through some more papers and put them on Denis's desk "I think it's probably true. I've done some investigating … there's confirmation here that he was deported from England over a year ago and will never be allowed to return – he had no work permit and there is unconfirmed suspicion that he was involved in child trafficking."

"So she can't go to him." Denis agreed. "What do you recommend, Judith?"

Judith leaned forward eagerly, glancing round at her colleagues. "I recommended that Abela should be allowed to stay in England in the care of the social services. I think she should be placed for adoption as soon as possible."

She sat back and closed her eyes, and she felt again the sweltering heat of the African sun, the chant of excited voices as boys ran to greet her bus with their trays of fruit and cakes, and the little girl holding a strip of material over her mother's head to give her some shade. She could hear her colleagues murmuring round her, discussing Abela's case. None of them knew Abela, yet her future was in their hands.

At last the committee came to a decision. They agreed that Abela should be placed for adoption, but not that she should be kept in England.

"It's not in her best interests," Denis said, as Judith started to protest. "She's only lived here for six months. I think we agree." He glanced round at the others in the team. "We should make arrangements for her to be repatriated so that the Tanzanian social services can place her for adoption in her own country."

Judith Carrington could have cried with frustration.

5 **to investigate** to try and find out the truth – 7 **work permit** [ˈpɜːmɪt] document that gives sb permission to work – 8 **suspicion** [səsˈpɪʃən] a feeling that sb is doing sth (usually sth bad or wrong) – 8 **child trafficking** [ˈtræfɪkɪŋ] illegal trade with children – 10 **to recommend** [rekəˈmend] to advise – 28 **to repatriate** [riːˈpætrieɪt] to take or send sb back to his/her own country

Chapter 19

ROSA

We never really expected to see Molly again, which was sad because I had come to really like her, with her faded, hippy clothes and her spectacular shoes. But after Anthony left, we put all thoughts of adoption behind us. We had tried and failed, Mum said. Never again.

So when Molly came round, Mum greeted her politely and asked her in, but she didn't offer her a cup of tea, and they didn't chat like old friends. I know she blamed Molly because the adoption had fallen through; I think she felt that if Molly had been more thorough, Anthony would never have been placed for adoption in the first place.

"I've just come to see if you'd like me to keep your name on the books," Molly said.

I clenched and unclenched my fingers. And Mum said no. She didn't look at me, didn't look at Molly. Her face was white.

"That's it then," said Molly, folding up her wallet. "Gosh, the end of the story. I'm so sorry, Jen. You have a lot to offer. Let me know if you ever change your mind."

"I won't," Mum said. "That's it now."

But life is full of little miracles, Nana says, and not long after all that, something totally unexpected happened, and it's changed our lives again.

We were at Ice Sheffield. I was really nervous about going skating again and it was all I could do to get myself laced up and ready for action. Mum held my hand and we did a whole

4 **faded** dull, greyish – 6 **to fail** to be unsuccessful – 10 **to blame** to say that sb is responsible for sth bad – 12 **thorough** ['θʌrə] careful *(gründlich)* – 18 **wallet** folder, file – 22 **miracle** sth very good that happens — so good that it is unbelievable *(Wunder)*

circuit together, slow and steady, and then she said, "You'll be fine, Off you go now." She let go; and I was free; I could do it, I was myself again. It was a great feeling, skimming in and out between the other skaters; I felt completely confident again. I slowed down to get my breath back, and did a gentle spin, and that was when I saw the little boy in the middle of the rink, right in the glowing square of sunlight that came through the window. He had no style whatsoever. He was completely fearless. He was laughing across at me. I could hardly believe it; I daren't believe it.

"Anthony!" I shouted.

He flung his arms wide, lunging towards me like a dog let off its leash, and I just caught him before he catapulted into me. I lifted him right up and hugged him, tight, tight. We were all laughing, Anthony, me and Mum, and then the man who I recognised as Anthony's father glided up towards us, slow and easy and smiling, and stopped right next to us, neat as a cat. I think that this is the best day of my life. So far.

1 **circuit** ['sɜːkɪt] circle – 12 **to lunge** [lʌndʒ] to make a sudden movement – 13 **leash** *Leine*

Chapter 20

ABELA

Eventually the Tanzanian social services wrote to Judith Carrington to say they did not want to take Abela into their care. They had thousands of homeless children to care for, they told her, and though it was the way of Tanzanian families just to accept homeless relatives into their midst, there were still too many children to find homes for.

Another case conference was called, and Judith took the letter and read it aloud to Denis and her colleagues. 'In our opinion, it would be in Abela's best interest to stay in England, if a suitable home could be found for her. We would be happy to support Miss Carrington's suggestion that Abela could be placed for adoption in England.' Judith put the letter down and looked round at the other social workers.

"She's a very, very brave child," she said. "But I think she's been through enough. She's been abandoned. I'd like to find an adoptive family for her as soon as possible."

"Well," said the team-leader at last. "We can see that Abela is a special case. If residence in this country is granted, we'll take her case to the next adoption panel."

He smiled at her. "Any more clients to discuss?"

"They're not *clients*," Judith said, as she did at every meeting. "They're *children*. And I have forty on my books." Forty young lives, and they were all in her care, all special cases. "All needing hope."

7 **midst** *here:* group, community – 13 **suggestion** [sə'dʒestʃən] idea – 17 **to abandon sb** to leave sb behind – 20 **residence** *Wohnrecht* – 20 **to grant** to permit, allow – 21 **panel** jury, board of people who decide

Chapter 21

ROSA

It was a gorgeous summer that year, a summer of trips into Derbyshire, picnics at Padley Gorge and camping out at Edale, swimming in the open-air pool at Hathersage, cycling round Ladybower. Nana and Grandpa usually came with us, and, sometimes, Anthony and his father. He says we're an important part of Anthony's little life and he wants us to keep in touch with him. But I've seen the way he looks at Mum, and I've seen the way Mum looks at him. Nana sees it too, and no one says anything to anybody. Funny, isn't it? It's like a little candle just flickering in a still room. Don't breathe, or it might go out. Sometimes I daydream about us all living in the same house, but I don't mention it to a soul.

So when Mum said to me one day, "Rosa, come over here a minute, I've got something very special to ask you," I thought, this is it. The candle gleamed brightly for a moment and I hitched up a grin all over my face. But it wasn't that.

"How would you feel if we contacted Molly again?" she asked me. "I'm ready to try again."

4 **Derbyshire** ['dɑ:bɪʃə] English county *(Grafschaft)* – 4 **Padley Gorge** valley in the Peak District – 4 **Edale** ['i:deɪl] village in the Derbyshire Peak District, a mountainous area – 5 **Hathersage** ['hæðəseɪdʒ] village in the Peak District – 6 **Ladybower** ['leɪdibaʊə] *(Reservoir)* lake in the Peak District – 18 **to hitch up a grin** to pretend to smile

Chapter 22

ABELA

Abela knew nothing about all these meetings and case conferences, letters and phone calls that were going on. All she knew was that Mrs Oladipo talked to her more and was kinder to her. Mr Oladipo listened to her read every night after school, and chuckled deep in his belly when she got things wrong, and clapped his long flapping fingers together when she got them right. Cathy and Lola ignored her mostly, but they never teased her or bullied her. Lola was soon to be leaving the Oladipos', and she and Cathy were as close as sisters now, dreading the parting.

During the school summer holidays Jasmine phoned Abela to invite her to tea. Immediately, Abela ran upstairs and changed out of the yellow and green clothes that Carmel liked her to wear, into her kanga. She came downstairs with Mrs Long's cardigan draped over her arm. For the first time since she had left the hospital, she was smiling.

"I'm sorry, but you can't go," Carmel told her.

Abela stared at her, her mouth open, her smile half-fading.

"No good looking at me like that," Carmel said. "You're in my care, Abela. I can't just let you go into any strange houses."

"Please," whispered Abela. She was beginning to tremble with a strange passion that she couldn't understand.

"No," Carmel said. "You can't. I'm your Mum while you're with me. I'm saying no."

It was then that Abela did something that she had never done before, that she did not even know how to do. She screamed, and she went on screaming, so loud and long that the sound seemed to come out of the walls of the house, down the stairs, through the windows, every brick and stone and pane of glass screamed with her. She threw herself on the ground and beat the rug with her fists, and when Mr Oladipo tried to lift her up she kicked out at him, twisting and turning violently, screaming, bellowing, yelling, raging with all the power and strength that her body possessed. There was no holding her down or quietening her, there was no comforting, there was only her pent-up rage, billowing and gathering and finally bursting out of her.

Carmel told me a few days later that Miss Carrington had been to see Jasmine's mother and father and said I could go and have tea there.

I think she wanted me to smile, but I didn't.

"Actually, Jasmine's Mum asked if you could stay overnight."

My insides bumped, but I still didn't smile.

"You can if you want. It's all right with me."

Jasmine came with her father in their big black car to collect me. This time I knew my smile was coming but I didn't give it to Carmel or The Dad, I saved it for Jasmine. We sat in the back of the car and held hands and I let my smile out then. In the house I couldn't stop giggling, and neither could Jasmine. There were so many children that nobody noticed us giggling. We went up to bed straight after tea and tried each other's clothes on and giggled, and Jasmine brought her mother's beads in and we put them on, in our hair and round our neck and our wrists and our ankles, and we danced and shimmered and watched ourselves in the glass and giggled. We talked and whispered and laughed long after the other children and Jasmine's parents had gone to bed.

And when I went back to Carmel's house I told her, "Jasmine's my sister."

She laughed down at me, her big wet laugh.

1 **pane of glass** window – 3 **rug** *Teppich* – 5 **to bellow** ['beləʊ] to shout loudly – 6 **to possess** [pə'zes] to have – 8 **pent-up** *aufgestaut* – 8 **to billow** ['bɪləʊ] to rise – 15 **to bump** to move up – 26 **ankle** part of the body between the foot and leg

"All my girls want sisters if they don't have them," she said. "And if they do have them, they wish they hadn't!"

"I'm going to live at her house when I leave here," I said. I looked at Carmel sideways. I wondered if I was going to scream again, like that other time when all the house screamed back at me. I wondered what she would do if I did, whether she would hate me or hit me or send me away. I lifted up my fists ready to beat her and she bent down to me and said,

"One day soon, Miss Carrington's going to find you a lovely family to live with. But till then, I'm your Mum, Abela, and this is your family. I'm taking care of you, as if you were one of my own."

Lola was moving to live with a cousin and his wife who ran a hotel in the Lake District. On the day she left there was a party for her. Carmel made a sponge cake and showed Abela how to smear the chocolate icing over it with the back of a knife.

"Abela helped to make this," Carmel announced at teatime.

Lola slid something across the table to Abela, wrapped up in kitchen paper. It was the key ring that Susie had given her. Later, Lola stood in the sunshine garden in a new dress and smiled for Mr Oladipo's camera. Soon her picture would be on the wall with all the other children who had stayed in the house. When she was leaving, she and Cathy clung to each other, sobbing.

"I hate it," Cathy said. "It's always the same. I just get used to someone, and they go back home, or they get adopted, or they go to another foster home, or I have to move. I hate it! I hate it!"

Mrs Oladipo spent a lot of time with her that night, while Abela and Mr Oladipo washed up the dishes in silence. And it was different without Lola, loud, shouting, tempestuous Lola.

14 **Lake District** area in northern England with many lakes – 15 **sponge cake** light cake that looks and feels like a sponge (but tastes better!) – 16 **icing** sweet, sugary mixture on the top of a cake *(Kuchenglasur)* – 31 **tempestuous** [tem'pestjuəs] difficult, involving strong emotions

To her dismay, Abela was moved back into the big room with Cathy.

"I'm sorry, but I've got a boy coming next," Mrs Oladipo said. "He'll need that little yellow room you've got. And anyway, Cathy won't be here for much longer. She's promised me she's going to study hard now, to go into nursing. She'll be no bother."

Abela shrank into herself again. She had loved the yellow room. The big room was echoey and the curtains flapped noisily at night, Cathy talked in her sleep and sulked when she was awake. And Abela was afraid, realising now that it was true; nobody stayed with the Oladipos for very long. What was going to happen to her?

Towards the end of the summer holidays, she heard Miss Carrington's voice in the garden and ran outside to meet her. Last time Miss Carrington had seen her Abela had been shy and withdrawn, saying little, watching every movement with huge, frightened eyes, but never looking anyone in the face. Now she ran to Miss Carrington and held her hand, pulling her into the kitchen to show her the latest book she was reading, telling her the story of what had happened so far.

"Wait, hold on, poor Miss Carrington doesn't have to hear every word!" Mrs Oladipo laughed.

"You've done well," the social worker told Mrs Oladipo. "She's a different child now."

"She doesn't have nightmares no more," Mrs Oladipo said. "And her sheets are always dry, aren't they Abela? And," she pinched Abela's tummy, "she eats like a horse!"

Abela giggled and squirmed away from her.

"Well, I've come with good news for you both," Miss Carrington said. "First, Abela is now a resident of England. That means you can stay in this country for as long as you want, Abela."

1 **dismay** [dɪs'meɪ] huge disappointment – 6 **to go into nursing** to become a nurse – 10 **to sulk** to be in a bad mood *(schmollen)* – 17 **withdrawn** shy and quiet – 28 **to pinch** *kneifen* – 28 **tummy** *(inf)* stomach – 31 **resident** ['rezɪdənt] sb who lives in a country legally

Abela frowned. "I still go to Tanzania when I'm a doctor?"

"Of course you can! And I'm sure you will. But that's a long time away, Abela. Meanwhile we have to find somewhere for you to live."

Abela looked anxiously at Mrs Oladipo. This was the news she had been dreading. "But I live here."

"Yes, you do, but Mr and Mrs Oladipo are foster parents. You know what that means? It means they just look after you for a bit while we find a family who will be yours for all your life."

"I want to stay here."

"Ooh, I'll be an old lady soon," Mrs Oladipo said. "You need a proper mum and dad with a bit more energy than me and The Dad have got."

"I promise you won't leave here till I've found exactly the right family for you, one we both like." Judith smiled at Abela. "All children should have a family to look out for them and look after them when they're growing up. I want you to trust me. I want you to be happy."

Abela nodded, biting her lip, feeling the burn of tears behind her eyes. But she did trust her. She was the one who had helped her mother, long ago and far away in Africa.

"You'll meet them and get to know them first. You'll see photos of them, and they'll see photos of you, even before you meet them. And if you don't like them, you don't go there."

Abela fiddled with the zip of her green jacket. Carmel hummed noisily at the sink. She had been through this so many times, easing her children into being strong enough to be taken away from her. So strange, so painful, every time.

"I've got something here for you," Miss Carrington said. She brought a red hardbacked notebook out of her bag. "I'm going to help you to write this. It will be your life story book."

"My life story?" Abela was mystified.

"Everything you can remember about your life can go in this. And you'll keep it forever. Shall we start now?"

Abela nodded at her solemnly, and Mrs Oladipo stood up. “I’ve got beds to make,” she said. “We’ve got the new boy coming tomorrow. Sammy, he’s called. Nice name. I’ll leave you two to get on with it.”

Miss Carrington opened the book. “Shall I write it, or you, Abela? This is going to have everything you want to say in it. You can draw pictures in it, and put photographs in, and write any memories you want to write. You don’t have the start at the beginning, Start anywhere you like. Write anything you like.”

Abela took the book and opened it carefully. She stroked the cool, smooth pages. “Now?” she asked.

Miss Carrington nodded. “Yes, let’s start now. I’ve brought you a special pencil.” She gave her a pencil that glittered when she turned it, and had an eraser at the end.

For a long time they sat in silence.

“It’s hard for you to remember when you were a baby,” Miss Carrington said. “Shall we start with a best memory? Something about your mama, something you and Mama loved doing together.”

Abela’s eyes went misty with concentration. “We have a game,” she said at last.

“Good. Tell me about your game.”

And so, very slowly, Abela began to write. Sometimes she asked Miss Carrington how to say something, or how to spell it, and every now and again she would stop and read it out loud, and Miss Carrington would help her to put down the next bit. This was how her Life Story began, though it was not the beginning of her life. Maybe she was about four years old when this first happened.

We have a game, Mamma and I, when we pound maize. When the corncobs have been drying in the sun for long enough, we shake off all the little yellow buds into a heap, and we pour them into a basket. They go tchick, tchick, as they trickle down.

20 **misty** foggy

Then we grind the buds into flour. We pound it with the end of a long stick from a tree, which is just as tall as Mama. It takes so long that our legs ache and ache with standing and our arms are heavy with holding the branch and stamping it down again and again. We must do it for hours, every day when the corn is ripe, to make enough for our food, to make enough to sell. The sky is greasy and sweaty. Flies buzz round my face and walk on my skin, and because my hands are busy I can't brush them away. They crawl in my hair and I can't do anything about them. My head throbs and I'm thirsty and tired.

This is when the game starts. Just when I think I can't do any more, Mama shouts, "One, Abela!" She raises her branch and then she let go of it and she claps her hands before she catches it again.

After a bit, Miss Carrington stood up and crept out, and Abela didn't even notice, because she was lost in her memories.

Now that the panel had agreed that Abela should be placed for adoption, Miss Carrington wanted it to happen as soon as possible. She looked through the lists of potential adopters in her area and found no one suitable, no one who wanted a child of Abela's age. Tanzanian girl, age nine. Nobody quite fitted the bill.

It was late, and she was tired, but memories of Abela kept flitting through her mind. Abela propping up her mother to help her out of the bus. Abela lying in hospital, closed up against the world that had taken her mother, father, baby sister and grandmother away from her. Abela laughing and skipping out to meet her that morning. Abela lost in a daydream of memories.

She had three more letters to read in her file, and then she would go home. One had been sent when she was still abroad

19 **potential** [pəˈtentʃəl] possible

and had never been brought to her notice. It came from a colleague in Sheffield, Molly West.

'We have a client looking for a Tanzanian child, preferably a girl, preferably Junior school age.'

Judith looked at her watch and picked up the phone. Molly West might have finished work for the day, but she might just be working late, like Judith. It was worth a try. Her hand rested on the receiver, and then withdrew. Was it fair to nail down a family for Abela yet? The little girl was very plucky, she was coping well, but she still had a lot of grief to work through. What if the placement turned out to be unsuitable? It was unthinkable to risk moving her somewhere that wasn't right for her. And Sheffield was so far away, it would be hard for her to keep up regular visits while the pre-adoption placement was happening.

And yet it was so hard to find a family willing to adopt a girl of Abela's age, particularly if she was from another culture. She looked at Molly's letter again. It was three months since she had sent it. This family was probably fixed up by now. Anything at all could have happened in the meantime. Yet could she risk missing a chance like this? She tidied up her desk for the night and left the letter from Molly on the top. She would sleep on it, she decided.

4 **Junior school** upper part of primary school (for children aged 8 to 11) – 8 **to withdraw sth** to take sth away – 8 **to nail down** *here:* to decide on, to determine – 9 **plucky** *(inf)* brave – 10 **to cope** to get along *(zurechtkommen)* – 17 **particularly** [pəˈtɪkjələli] especially – 21 **to tidy up** to clean and put things into order

Chapter 23

ROSA

On a wet day, soon after the new school term started, I came home to find Molly having tea with Mum. I was so pleased to see her again that I went up and hugged her, just like I do with all my favourites of Mum's friends. She was holding a photograph. A little girl of nine or ten looked solemnly up at me. She had her face cocked slightly to one side, like a bird, and her fingers made a little tent under her chin.

"Who's that?" I asked casually. My heart was doing its pumpity-pump excited dance. *Little sister, little sister*, my blood sang in my ears. *Little sister, little sister.*

"Her name is Abela Mbisi," said Molly. "I've just been telling your mum about her. I've been sent her details from the adoption services in London. She's been through a terrible time, this little girl."

She passed the photograph across to Mum.

"It's so important to find the right home for her, as soon as possible. She needs so much love and a secure home. And of course, the first people I thought about were you two. She fits your initial application absolutely, and no one else in my area has made a similar request. I just wondered if you would like to come and meet her." I hardly dared look at Mum.

"There is one problem, that I have to tell you now," Molly went on. "Her parents both died of HIV Aids. We have no way of knowing whether Abela has Aids herself, or is a carrier. She may be. She can't be tested without her parents' consent, and they're dead. I have to tell you this."

14 **to send details** [ˈdiːteɪlz] **to sb** to inform sb – 19 **secure** safe – 22 **to make a similar request** to ask sb almost the same thing – 23 **hardly** almost not *(kaum)* – 25 **we have no way of knowing** we do not know at all – 26 **to be a carrier** to be infectious – 27 **consent** permission

The silence went on forever. I knew exactly what Mum was thinking. I knew a lot about Aids from television programmes and school. I knew that it was a terrible problem, particularly in parts of Africa. What if that little girl did have Aids? What if she died of it? To adopt a child and lose her would be more than Mum could bear. But I knew what else she was thinking. To give a chance of happiness to someone in this situation is a rare gift. It doesn't happen very often. I went and stood behind her, touching her just lightly on the shoulder. It's what she does to me sometimes, when I need a bit of support.

"Yes," said Mum at last. "I'll come and meet her."

8 **gift** present

Chapter 24

ABELA

Abela spent hours writing in her book, slowly and painfully, struggling to write in English as much as in Swahili, struggling to bring her memories to the surface. When she wasn't writing there was a voice in her head, framing the words that she would later struggle to put on the page. She felt she was talking aloud to someone when she was writing, someone who understood her and wanted to be her friend.

"Want any help?" Carmel asked to her one day. She worried that Abela was spending so much time up in her room on her own.

"I write my life story," Abela said shyly. "But I can't remember everything."

"Show me some of the things you brought with you. Show me your pretty kangas! I bet they've got stories to tell!"

Abela ran upstairs and brought her two kangas down and spread them on the table. "They've got words printed on them," Carmel said. "Can you tell me what they mean?"

"This one mean 'You will remember me'," said Abela shyly. "And this one mean 'Be my friend'."

"Oh, I'd like one that says, 'Come and do my housework!" Carmel laughed. "Where can I buy it? Marks and Spencers?"

Abela giggled. "We have a big market, where they sell them. They sell everything there. All kinds fruit, chickens, beans. And cloths like this. Some is bright cotton like this. And some is not heavy, like the Asian ladies wear."

"Oh, don't I love markets! Tell me what it was like, Abela. Did your Mum sell things there?"

5 **to bring to the surface** ['sɜːfɪs] to retrieve, to bring up so that sth can be seen – 16 **I bet** I am sure – 23 **Marks and Spencers** big British department store chain

Abela nodded. She closed her eyes and swayed on the balls of her feet as she described the shady, covered stalls of the main market and the open square where she and her mother and the poorest women used to sit. She told about the little mounds of oranges and bananas, red beans, chilli peppers, the live chickens, the thieving dogs and cats. She flicked her eyes open dramatically and told Carmel about the mad mzee with her curved, deadly panga, chasing the children and the teacher round the stalls. Carmel shrieked with laughter.

"I write now," Abela said.

"Ok, my love. I'll leave you to it."

Another time, on one of the social worker's visits, Abela showed Judith Carrington the sloppy sandals and told her about Bibi's friend who had given them to her.

"What's she like? Abela? Can you see her in your mind?"

Abela frowned, trying to catch the slippery picture before it disappeared. "She fat. She has a bit of tooth missing, here. She cooks good mayai."

"Mayai, that's egg, isn't it? I remember that."

Abela chuckled. "Mayai yanayavonigua."

"My goodness! You've got me there! What's that?"

Abela flicked her fingers together rapidly.

"Oh, I know! Scrambled egg!" They both laughed. "You'd better put that in your book, Abela. Can't have you forgetting a word like that!"

After she had written it down, giggling again as they tried to imagine how to spell it, Abela let the pencil roll away from her. She sat with her head bowed, clenching and unclenching her fingers.

"Is there something else about her?" Judith asked.

Slowly, half-whispering, Abela told her then how Bibi and the same friend had held her down under the flame tree while

1 **to sway** to move from one side to the other – 5 **mound** [maʊnd] pile – 6 **thieving dogs** dogs who take away food – 23 **scrambled egg** *Rührei*

the medicine woman cut her. She described how she had been looking up at the blinding yellow sun but had been too frightened to close her eyes in case Bibi thought she was dead. She told how she had heard the green monkeys screaming and had wanted to put her own screams among them, but that Bibi's hand was pressed over her mouth so she couldn't make any scream at all. She told her about the angel wings beating about her head until everything was dark and peaceful. And afterwards, how Bibi and her friend had taken it in turns to wash her with water scented with healing herbs, and had sung to her in their deep warm red voices.

The social worker did not write this down. When Abela had finished talking she closed up the book and said, "You've remembered that very well Abela. I wonder if you're angry with Bibi for letting it happen?"

Abela was silent, clenching her fists until her knuckles were white. She felt her screams rising inside her, then spreading out, dissolving. She nursed her top lip inside her bottom teeth. Then she nodded. Her tears scalded her eyes.

"Well, you know, I don't think Bibi wanted to hurt you. She did it because she thought it was the right thing to do to girls; the same thing happened to her, and to her mother, and her mother before that. But many people realise now that it is not a good thing to do, and they're able to stop doing it."

"When I'm a doctor, I'll tell them," Abela said.

"That's right," Judith smiled. "When you're a doctor, they'll listen to you. You'll be a wise woman!"

"I am wise," Abela nodded thoughtfully. "I think I am ten years old now."

"Really? When was your birthday?"

Abela shrugged. "I don't know. But I think I am ten now."

"Well, that's quite old. D'you think you're too old to play Snakes and Ladders with Cathy?"

10 **scented** ['sentɪd] **with** carrying the smell of – 10 **healing herbs** [hɜːbz] *Heilkräuter* – 16 **knuckle** ['nʌkəl] part of your hand *(Knöchel)* – 18 **to dissolve** to disappear – 19 **to scald** [skɔːld] to burn – 33 **Snakes and Ladders** board game (snakes are bad, ladders are good)

"I love Snakes and Ladders!" Abela giggled. "I'll even play it when I'm as old as Bibi!"

Judith persuaded Cathy to come down and have a break from her homework. She stumped downstairs, moaning that her brain was hurting, and Carmel produced her battered compendium of games from the cupboard by the fireplace.

"Do I have to?" Cathy moaned, but she caught Carmel's look, raised her eyebrows in despair and slid down onto the chair next to Abela. In minutes Abela's mood had changed; she was bright and quick with laughter, full of the fun of the game. Judith tidied the objects that Abela had brought downstairs to write about, and flicked through the animal book that Abela and Susie had made.

"What a lovely book – but who scribbled in it?" she asked. "Was it you, Abela?"

"It was me," said Cathy, blushing to the roots of her hair. "Me and Lola."

"Then you can just rub them out," Carmel said. "What a mess!"

She took the book and opened it at the last page. "What's this?" she asked.

Judith studied the certificate for a moment, and then smiled and nodded. "It's just about the most important piece of paper Abela could have," she said. "It's going to save us all a great deal of anguish. Fancy it being here all the time! I'll look after it for her now." She prised up the sellotape that Susie had used, and put the HIV Aids certificate carefully in her folder. Then she gave Cathy the book.

"Do your best with it," she told her. "It's precious."

She paused in the doorway for a moment, watching the girls with their heads bent together over the board game, then went out to her car. Carmel followed her out.

6 **compendium** collection – 16 **to blush** to turn red in the face – 25 **anguish** ['æŋgwɪʃ] great pain – 29 **precious** ['preʃəs] valuable, worth a lot

"She's such a plucky kid!" Carmel said. "I don't think I've ever come across a child who's been through so much, and I probably don't know the half of it."

"The main thing is, she's coming through it. Every time I see her she looks better. You're doing very well with her, Carmel."

"I love that child," Carmel admitted. "Don't say that about all of them, do I? Glad to see the back of some of them, however hard I've tried." She shook her head, laughing, wiping her eyes with the back of her hand. "But this little one ... We got off to a bad start, and it was my fault. Never looked after a little girl before. But we're ok now. The Dad thinks as much of her as I do. Let's hope nothing else goes wrong in her life. Will someone adopt her?"

"At her age, who can tell? But I have made a contact, I think." Judith looked down at her notes. "Six more children to visit today, and they've all got their own problems. I'd better get a move on!"

After that, Carmel helped Abela to write in her book every day, while Cathy was doing her homework. It was the quiet time, she said. Time to sit down and rest her feet.

"My toes are like big balloons, just look at them! Go on now, tell me the story of your long life!" she would say to Abela. "What've you got to show me today?"

Abela would run upstairs and sort through her things in the bedside cupboard; sometimes she would choose Mrs Long's cardigan or the beaded mirror key ring, or the book of animals that she and Susie had drawn. It was some time before she chose the Coca-Cola car.

"This my best thing," she told Carmel. "My Baba make me this car."

"Ah, now you tell me, I can see it's meant to be a car!" Carmel tried to make the squashed wheels turn on the tabletop. "But I

32 **to squash** to press into a flat shape

must say it just looks like a battered old tin can. Shall we write about this today?"

"Me write!" said Abela, putting on a baby voice. She loved this time, this special time of day that was just for her.

"Say it properly."

"I'll write it." Abela giggled.

"That's better. Write about your Daddy."

Abela's eyes clouded. It was so long now since her father died. His face slid in and out of her memory, like a fish drifting in and out of shadowed water. She couldn't hold it there. She couldn't see him.

"Was he like The Dad?" Carmel prompted. "Like a great quiet grizzly grumpy old bear?" She hooted with laughter.

Abela shook her head. 'Baba is a big, strong man,' she wrote. 'He is my father. He has walked many miles and he has climbed many hills. But he has not been to England. He has not been to any town. He has not been on a bus.' She stared in to space, trying to see again the man who was her father, trying to smell his warm skin and feel the soft touch of his hands on her face, trying to hear the brown rumble of his singing in church. 'He has a black cow called Yetu and he could sing like Yetu." Abela giggled. She deepened her voice and mooed like a cow. "Lovely big voice. And he made me this car."

She held the car in both her hands, remembering how Baba had shaped the wheels by cutting pieces of tin and flattening them with a stick, curling the strips round a little rod. She could hear his slow, thoughtful breathing as he worked, rumbling his Yetu song to make her laugh; she could see again how he had squatted on his haunches to make the car roll on the ground for the very first time. But now the Coco-Cola tin body was squashed and scratched, the wheels were flattened and useless. She put the car down and took up her pencil again.

13 **grumpy** bad-tempered, easily annoyed – 28 **Yetu** Swahili for "our". *Baba yetu* is the Swahili name for The Lord's Prayer *(das Vaterunser)*. – 29 **to squat on your haunches** *(hin)hocken*

Carmel went outside to speak to her husband, who was prising caterpillars off his cabbages. After a bit he came into the kitchen carrying the toolbox from the shed. While Abela was writing he took up her car and began to prise the flattened wheels from the bodywork, coiling them round to make them roll again. Carmel sent Cathy to the local shop to buy a tin of Coke, then poured it out for them to share, grinning at each other because fizzy drinks were usually forbidden, hiccupping as it went down too fast. The Dad fixed the wheels onto the new Coke tin, testing it from time to time on the tabletop by rolling it carefully backwards and forwards. During all this time he never spoke a word, just whistled very slightly between his teeth like a sissing snake, but when he had finished he handed the car to Abela and said, "This isn't as good as the way your daddy made it. I'm all thumbs these days."

And at that moment Carmel snapped her camera and there was Abela, clutching her new car and smiling with joy.

The next time Miss Carrington visited, Abela was writing about the red cardigan and the yellow echoey schoolhouse in Tanzania. In her daydreams insects buzzed and hummed around her head, a laughing jackass shrieked in the trees outside, children chanted their tables as Mrs Long wrote them out on the board. 'Mrs Long has curly black hair,' she wrote. 'Mrs Long is so kind.'

"Would you like to write a letter to your teacher?" Judith asked her. "I'm sure we can find a way of getting it to her. She'd love to know how you are, Abela."

"Can I?" Abela's eyes were wide with surprise.

Carmel brought her a piece of writing paper and Abela stared at it for a long time, as if she expected words to appear on it by magic.

"Dear Mrs Long," Carmel prompted her.

2 **caterpillar** ['kætəpɪlə] small creature that turns into a butterfly – 2 **cabbage** ['kæbɪdʒ] vegetable *(Kohl)* – 8 **fizzy** with gas – 15 **I'm all thumbs** *(inf)* not to be able to do difficult work which involves one's fingers

Abela licked her lips carefully and wrote, "Dear Missus Long." then she looked up. "What else will I write?" she whispered.

"Anything," Judith said. "What would you say to her if you met her in the street now?"

"Hello Teacha. How are you?" Abela said shyly. She began to write, 'I am very well. I am very happy. I have a friend called Jasmine and a friend called Carmel and a friend called Cathy and The Dad who mend my car is my friend and I have a friend called Judith and she is my,' she paused, 'soshal werker. I see her in Africa. Abela."

Judith read the letter and smiled. "Do you know, Abela, this will make Mrs Long very, very happy. I'll find out where to send it and I'll post it today. Now, I've got something important to tell you."

"Uh oh! Cup of tea time!" Carmel sang. She went over to the sink and closed her eyes tight. This was the moment she longed for and dreaded with every child who came into her care.

"You know we've talked in the past about *one day*, when you'll move on to live with a new family, the family you'll stay with for the rest of your life?" Judith asked.

Abela nodded solemnly. She could see Carmel, standing by the sink with her back to her. It was as if a chasm was opening up between them, dark and deep and frightening. Miss Carrington's voice was coming to her from far away, from the other side of her world, the other side of her life.

"Well, we've found someone who might be just right. Tomorrow a lady is coming to see you. She's looking for a little girl just like you to adopt, and she'd like to meet you."

Carmel turned round, smiling encouragement at her. "That's lovely, honey. Someone who can give you a nice home for your life. You're ready for a nice family all of your own."

8 **to mend** to repair – 17 **to dread** [dred] to be afraid of – 22 **chasm** ['kæzəm] huge gap *(Abgrund)* – 29 **encouragement** [ɪn'kʌrɪdʒmənt] support, help

"No promises on either side," Judith told her. "Just meet her and see if you like her. I won't let you go anywhere if you're not happy with the idea. But I'd like you to meet her."

"But I don't want." Abela stared down at her letter to Mrs Long. She remembered her teacher's words, "Be happy, Abela." She had wondered then if she could ever be happy again, and since then she had often wondered whether there was anyone in the world she could trust. But now she was beginning to be happy again, and she could trust Miss Carrington and Carmel. If they thought it was a good thing to meet this lady, then she must do it.

"I've brought a photograph of her." Judith took a picture out of her bag, and Abela looked sideways at it, the smiling, friendly face, the floppy brown hair. She looked kind.

"Her name's Jen Warren. There isn't a daddy in the house," Judith went on. "Just this lady and her daughter. This is Rosa."

"She is like me," Abela whispered, surprised.

"Well, she is. A bit like you. Her daddy came from Tanzania too."

Abela held the photograph in her hands. She turned it over, and then looked at it again, at the happy, friendly smiling face of the girl who might become her big sister.

"All right," she whispered. "I try."

But as soon as Miss Carrington had gone she burst into tears. Carmel stood with her arms round her, rocking her gently backwards and forwards, backwards and forwards.

"There, there, she said. "You cry honey, you cry. That's real good. That's real good."

Chapter 25

ROSA

And that was how my little sister came to live with us. It seems like ages ago now; it feels as if she has always lived here. But it was ages before it all happened. I couldn't believe how long it took, all those meetings, all those talks. Mum met her, and I met her, and she came for tea, and she came for a weekend, and she came skating with me and hated it and fell over and cried. She met Nana and Grandpa, and loved them. And at last she moved in with her little bag of belongings. I was so excited that day, so proud and nervous. I took her to meet some of my friends.

"This is my sister, Abela."

I'm used to saying that now.

Abela started at our local primary school, the one I used to go to, after Christmas. Mum met her every day and walked through the park with her, holding her hand. She had a three months' adoption leave just as if she'd had a new baby.

Abela didn't call her anything at first, but then she started calling her Mummy. That was strange, but nice too, and right. I taught her how to make apricot slices. At first Mum talked to her a lot in Swahili, and I felt really out of it, and so they started to teach it to me. It's like a secret language now, that the three of us share when we're out together. Often Mum talks to us both about Africa, but she always talks about the good things, the friendly people and the proud, strong women that she knew when she was there, the beautiful places she has seen in the towns and in the countryside. We'll go there, one day, very soon. Mum's already saving up. She, Abela and I are

18 **leave** extended time off work

going to Africa, to Tanzania, to Abela's country and to mine. It's our promise to each other, our holiday in Africa, and nothing, nothing is going to stop us doing it.

Her English is getting better all the time, but she likes me to do 'lessons' with her. I help her to write letters to Mrs Long and to Carmel. She's so funny, the way the tip of her tongue wriggles on her bottom lip when she's writing. She covers the letters with pictures of animals, birds, flowers, and kisses. Her friend Jasmine came to stay for a weekend, and they giggled and cried so much that I got fed up and moved into Anthony's room. It's still his room, he comes to stay occasionally. I haven't got anywhere of my own any more, just my own bed.

And then, Adoption Day came, in the Easter holidays. We all went to the County Court; Mum, Grandpa, Nana, me and Abela, and Judith Carrington and Molly and some other people who we didn't know. It wasn't a big exciting place like they have in TV courtroom dramas; it was just a sort of office. We all sat round the biggest, shiniest table I've ever seen, with the judge at one end. She wasn't at all frightening; a gentle-looking woman with droopy eyelids and amazing fluffy hair, just dressed in ordinary clothes, which was a bit disappointing. My stomach was doing its butterfly quaking, and goodness knows how Mum and Abela were feeling, holding hands next to me. But everyone smiled, the papers were signed, and it was all over in two minutes.

Abela asked the judge where her wig was, and the judge sent the clerk to fetch it and then put it on Abela's head and we took a photograph of her; one huge smile under a frosty grey wig. Grandpa called her the wise old bird after that.

So that's how she became my little sister. It still isn't easy, for me or for Mum or for her. I got jealous when Grandpa started to teach her piano, but as soon as she was adopted he bought

6 **the tip of her tongue wriggles** her tongue moves backwards and forwards – 20 **droopy** hanging down (she's tired) – 22 **goodness knows** *(inf)* who knows – 26 **wig** false hair that judges wear – 31 **jealous** *eifersüchtig*

her a guitar and paid for her to have lessons on that instead. She sings when she's playing, in a lovely high golden-yellow voice.

I love it when Mum and I go out together, skating or shopping, just us, and leave Abela with Nana. I love it when I go to Grandpa's on my own for my piano lesson. But I love it, too, when Abela and I do things together. She's so funny, she's got a giggle that's like a stream bubbling, and once she starts, I get it too. We drive Mum mad when we're giggling.

We squabble sometimes. I pull her hair and she scratches me. She wants to know my secrets. She hangs around listening when my friends come round, when I just want to be on my own with them and dance in our bedroom and have a good time and talk about the boys we're crazy about. It's a real drag, sometimes, having her around.

And I have a sense that deep down, she's wiser and cleverer than me, she knows things that I will never know and she has seen things that I will never see; she'll do things that I will never do. I look into the blackness of her eyes and I see wild creatures and unknown frightening places and unbearable sorrow. She has come through all those things; but they're part of her forever, they have made her what she is. I think she will become a great person.

I wouldn't be without her for anything. Not for anything in the world. She's my little sister. She belongs.

10 **to squabble** ['skwɒbəl] to argue – 14 **a drag** *(sl, inf)* annoying

Acknowledgements

A little girl called Halima made a great impression on me. This story is not about her, but it is because of her that I wanted to write it.

I talked to many people while I was writing *The Girl Who Saw Lions*, and would like to thank in particular Julie Jarman and Dolores Long for their advice about Tanzania; Tricia Murray-Leslie and Maria Oldroyd for their advice about adoption; Helen Kendal for her advice about asylum seekers; Pat Reed for showing me how to ice skate; and, of course, my partner Alan Brown for his enormous encouragement.

Berlie Doherty

Kibali
Lake Turkana
Morungole
Nimule
Moyale
Lodwar
Chalbi Desert
Arua
Gulu
Moroto
Lira
Mahagi
Djugu
Atura
Wajir
MONTS BLEU
UGANDA
Irumu
Lake Albert
Hoima
Lake Kyoga
Mt. Elgon
KENYA
Mbale
Kitale
Mubende
Beni
Jinja
Eldoret
Baringo
Kampala
Kakamega
Kisumu
Mt. Kenya
Nakuru
Chuka
Garissa
Lake Edward
Mbarara
Lake Victoria
Kisii
Sotik
Nyeri
Embu
Kabale
Nairobi
Tana
Bur
Byumba
Bukoba
Musoma
Kitui
Machakos
Kibuye
Kigali
Ukerewe I.
Witu
RWANDA
Serengeti Plain
Lake Natron
Kipini
Mwanza
Ungama Bay
Ngozi
Galana
Kilimanjaro
Bujumbura
Geita
Mt. Meru
Malindi
BURUNDI
Shinyanga
Lake Eyasi
Kahama
Takaungu
GREAT RIFT VALLEY
Mombasa
Vanga
Kondoa
Masai Steppe
Tanga
Tabora
Pemba I.
Handeni
Lake Tanganyika
TANZANIA
Manyoni
Pangani
Zanzibar I.
Sadani
Zanzibar
Kitunda
Dodoma
INDIAN OCEAN
Bagamoyo
Moba
Dar es Salaam
Mtakuja
Morogoro
Lake Rukwa
Ras Buyuni
Gt. Ruaha
Iringa
RUBEHA MTNS
Rufiji
Kipili
Mafia I.
Sumbawanga
Utete
Pweto
Mohoro
Kasanga
Chunya
Matandu
Kilwa Kivinje
Mbeya
Mporokoso
Njombe
Kawambwa
Liwale
Mchinja
Kasama
Lindi
Karonga
Luwingu
Chilumba
Manda
Chinsah
Quionga
Songea
Masasi
Lake Bengweulu
Tunduru
Palma
Rovuma
Mpika
Mocímboa da Praia
Bandawe
Mueda
Lake Nyasa
Lundazi
Mucojo
Macomia
ZAMBIA
Maniamba
Quissanga
Lugenda
Montepuez
Serenje
Ancuabe
Marrupa
Balama
Mecúfi
Lilongwe
Namapa
Luangwa
MALAWI
MOZAMBIQUE
Lúrio
Nacala
Furancungo
Entre Rios
Zumbo
Lake Chilwa
Nampula
Lago de Cabora Basse
Zambezi
Ligonha
Mogincual
Chicoa
Blantyre
Nhamarro
Erego
Tete
Angoche

Additional Texts

1. Tanzania and UK – national factfile

1. General

	Tanzania	UK
Location	Central East Africa	Group of islands in Western Europe
Land area (km²)	945,000	243,610
Population	43,739,000 (2009)	61,792,000 (2009)
Climate features	Tropical. Highlands: 10 - 20°C, rest: never below 20°C. Hot period: Nov - Feb. Rainy seasons: south: Dec - Apr; north: Oct - Dec and March - May	Mild winters and temperate summers (continental climate influenced by the Gulf Stream)
Geographical features	North: lakes and mountains. Central Tanzania: hot, flat plains. East: ca 1,000 km of humid coast. Islands: Pemba, Zanzibar.	No high mountains. The south is flatter than the north. Nowhere in the UK is further than 113 km from the sea!
Ethnic mix	Over 120 groups, main ones: Sukuma and Nyamwezi. Also: Hehe, Bena, Gogo, Haya. Also ca 70,000 Arabs and 10,000 Europeans	8 - 10 % of the population (5 - 6 million) is from non-White ethnic groups. 45 % of non-White people live in London
Main religions	Roughly one third Muslim, one third Christian and one third local, African religions	ca 5.5 % of the population: no religion. Christian: 25 %. Muslims: ca 1 %

	Tanzania	UK
Languages	Official lingua franca: Swahili. English used widely in education and legal systems	English. Also some: Urdu, Hindi, Punjabi, Gujarati and Celtic languages: Welsh, Scots Gaelic, Cornish
Gross domestic product (2009)	$ 57.4 billion (per capita: $1,416)	$2.183 trillion (per capita: $35,334)
%age of working population in agriculture	ca 80 %. Half of GDP is agriculture (Source: "Earthtrend", 2004)	1.7 % (2004. In 1980 the figure was 2.6 %) (Source: "Earthtrend", 2004)

2. Health

	Tanzania	UK
	Mortality rate of children under five: 12 %. Life expectancy: 50 years. Leading causes of death in children: malaria, in adults: HIV/AIDS	Mortality rate of children under five: 0.6 %. Life expectancy: 79 years.
HIV/ AIDS	1.4 million Tanzanians (ca 6 % of the adult population) live with AIDS. 70.5 % of these are 25 to 49 years old; 15 % are aged 15 - 24.	108,766 reported cases by June 2008 (ca 0.16 % of the population)
Doctors / 10,000 people*	less than 0.5 (2006)	21.4 (2002)

** Source: World Health Organisation, Global Health Observatory, found at: http://apps.who.int/ghodata/)*

3. Education

Tanzania

Education is officially compulsory for seven years, until children are 15, but in practice, it is not enforced. In 2002, primary schools became officially free of charge, but in practice, various school expenses (books, "upkeep of garden", etc), have to be paid. A report made in 2008, *Findings on the Worst Forms of Child Labor,* made by the U.S. Bureau of International Labor Affairs, estimates that 35% of 5-14 year-olds were working, mostly in agriculture, and thus not at school, at least not regularly. Although official figures cannot really be trusted, it is estimated that in 1997, the teacher to pupil ratio was one to 40, now it is one to 53, which shows that although more children go to school now than before, the state almost certainly cannot pay for it properly. All secondary schools are fee paying.

UK

Education is compulsory for all children from their fifth birthday to the last Friday in June of the school year in which they turn 16. This will be raised in 2013 to the year in which they turn 17 and in 2015 to the year in which they turn 18 (not Scotland).

Since 1998: "New Deal": maximum class size of 30 for 5-7 year olds.

3 **compulsory** [kəm'pʌlsəri] obligatory *(Pflicht)* – 5 **free of charge** does not have to be paid for *(umsonst)* – 6 **expenses** *Ausgaben* – 9 **to estimate** *schätzen* – 12 **ratio** ['reɪʃiːəʊ] *Verhältnis*

2. Children in public care in the UK: some facts and figures

60,900 children were in the care of local authorities on 31st March 2009

Gender

57% (34,600) of children looked after on 31st March 2009 were boys and 43% (26,300) were girls

Age

- 5% (3,200) of children in care on 31st March 2009 were under 1 year old
- 16% (9,500) were aged between 1 and 4
- 17% (10,500) were aged between 5 and 9
- 41% (24,800) were aged between 10 and 15
- 21% (12,900) were aged 16 and over

Placements

- 73% (44,200) of children in care on 31st March 2009 were living with foster carers
- 10% (6,200) were living in children's homes (includes secure units, children's homes and hostels)
- 7% (4,100) were living with their parents
- 4% (2,500) were placed for adoption
- 3% (1,720) were placed in residential schools or other residential settings

22 **residential school** boarding school

Unaccompanied Asylum Seeking Children
3,700 unaccompanied asylum seeking children in care on 31st March 2009. 87 % (3,200) were boys and 13 % (490) were girls.

Adoption Orders by date of entry in Adopted Children Register (England and Wales, 2002 - 2007)

2002	5,680
2003	4,818
2004	5,562
2005	5,558
2006	4,979
2007	4,637

NB Figures on adoption orders apply to adoptions by relatives and step–parents as well as adoptions from care

Adoptions from Care
3,300 children were adopted from care during the year ending 31st March 2009. 51 % (1,600) of children adopted during the year ending 31st March 2009 were boys and 49 % (1,600) were girls.

Age
The average age at adoption was 3 years 9 months. 2 % (80) of children adopted during the year ending 31st March 2009 were under 1 year old. 72 % (2,300) were aged between 1 and 4 years old. 23 % (760) were aged between 5 and 9 years old. 3 % (80) were aged between 10 and 15 years old.

1 **unaccompanied** [ˌʌnəˈkʌmpənid] **children** children traveling alone – 1 **asylum** [əˈsaɪləm] **seeking** *Asylbewerber* – 14 **average** [ˈævrɪdʒ] *durchschnittlich*

Adopters

92 % (3,000) children were adopted by couples and 8 % (270) by single adopters during the year ending 31st March 2009.

Waiting times

75.8 % children were placed for adoption within 12 months of best interest decision during the year ending 31st March 2009.

Source: British Association for Adoption & Fostering, at http://www.baaf.org.uk/info/stats/england.shtml

3. Lions in Tanzania

GUNS AND MAGIC: A bush doctor holds a lion claw used to fend off bad juju.

from National Geographic magazine, October 2006

In the pitch darkness of the hut, it took Salum Mohamed a moment to get his bearings. It was not quite midnight, and he'd been throttled from a deep sleep by frantic shrieking, the timbre of which seemed so surreal Mohamed couldn't be certain he wasn't dreaming. "What's wrong?" he called out, stumbling from his bed and groping about in the dark.

Mohamed's wife and three sons were all fine, but as he made his way toward the spot where his nephew, Hassani Dadi, normally slept, he found the screaming child in a most unusual predicament. Little Hassani was wedged among the branches and palm leaves that formed the only unfinished wall of the hut, a wall waiting to be sealed with mud like the rest. Strange, Mohamed thought. He tried to grab hold of the boy, to free him from the branches. That's when the attackers on the other side of the wall made themselves known. They began to roar.

Mohamed knew that lions had been active recently in the area. They had taken goats and dogs near the village of Simana, about an hour's walk from here, and that was never a good sign. Mohamed had just moved his family from Simana to this isolated outpost, though he knew the wisdom of that decision was debatable. On the one hand, his *shamba,* or farm field, was here and living close by meant he could better protect his maize, millet, and rice crops against marauding bushpigs and

3 **to fend off bad juju** juju is a word from West Africa that refers to the supernatural power of an object; to fend off means to stop or prevent – 5 **pitch** black – 6 **to get your bearings** ['beərɪŋz] to find out where you are – 7 **to throttle** to seize, to take away from – 7 **frantic shrieking** very shrill cry – 8 **timbre** tone – 14 **predicament** situation – 14 **wedged** caught, stuck – 16 **sealed** closed *versiegelt* – 24 **the wisdom was debatable** it was not clear if it was a good decision – 27 **millet** type of cereal *(Korn)*

monkeys, the bane of his existence. On the other hand, he and his family were all alone, surrounded by the dense thorn scrub characteristic of southern Tanzania, behind which you never knew what was lurking. In case of an emergency, they'd have to fend for themselves.

One of the lions now snarling on the other side of the wall had moments earlier shoved its massive paw through the branches near where Hassani slept and sunk its claws into the boy's left arm. Now it was yanking him through the wall. Mohamed bear-hugged Hassani and began pulling him back in as hard as he could. A fierce struggle ensued, but it was over in seconds as man and boy stumbled backward in the darkness. Hassani's spindly arm was gone. It had detached at the shoulder.

Mohamed tried to stay composed. He quickly tied a tourniquet to what little was left of Hassani's arm—the blood was gushing—but the boy was making bizarre groans and gurgles. The otherworldly sounds of death, Mohamed thought. He laid Hassani carefully in another room, one with four good walls, and then hurried with his family up a ladder and onto the rafters beneath the thatch roof. Once again the lions jammed their paws through the makeshift wall, trying to get inside. But the branches held. Mohamed guessed there were two lions, maybe more. All he knew for certain was that if they penetrated that wall he'd have to fight them, with only a machete. The thought terrified him. All night the cats circled the hut. Mohamed waited.

By sunrise the lions were gone. And, miraculously, little Hassani was still alive.

1 **bane** cause of great trouble – 2 **scrub** dry grassland – 4 **to lurk** to wait *(lauern)* – 11 **to ensue** to follow – 13 **spindly** ['spɪndli] very thin – 13 **detached** come off – 15 **composed** calm – 16 **tourniquet** ['tɜ:nɪkeɪ] elastic piece of cloth – 17 **to gush** to flow quickly – 21 **rafter** ['rɑ:ftə] wooden plank under roof – 22 **makeshift** improvised *(provisorisch)* – 26 **machete** [mə'ʃeti] long knife usually used for cutting corn or grass

Mohamed pedaled him on a bicycle several miles to the tarmac highway, where they caught a bus to the hospital in Lindi. The child survived.

It's an amazing story. Breathtaking. But as I listen to Mohamed tell it, by the flickering light of a lantern outside in the village, I realize that one piece of it bothers me.

"Why did you leave Hassani downstairs?" I ask.

He thinks on this. "I put him in a secure place," he says, vaguely.

"A secure place?"

"I thought he was going to die," he says, stone-faced. He repeats this. He stares past me. But he never directly answers the question. He never says he faced an impossible dilemma that January night in 2003. He never talks about the cruelties of war, which is what this is, of possibly having to make a brutal, *Sophie's Choice*–like decision. Was there simply no more room in the rafters? Had he made his nephew available to the killers to save the rest of his family? Of course, he owes me no explanation. Hell, lions had invaded the man's home. I'm in no position to judge him.

But there is one person who can judge Mohamed, and he does so, right in the middle of our interview. Little Hassani comes racing up out of the darkness and begins screaming at his uncle. Earlier he had refused to pose with Mohamed for a photograph, saying, "No one helped me that night. I was scared because no one helped me." Now he's livid. "You cannot tell this story!" he insists. "This is not your story! You should not do the interview!" He's a cute kid, short for a ten-year-old, not quite four feet tall. A small flap of skin dangles from the left sleeve of his T-shirt, but the larger wound, apparently, is emotional. He kicks the dirt in front of Mohamed before turning and running off into the night.

2 **tarmac** *asphaltiert* – 6 **to bother** to worry – 16 **Sophie's Choice** novel by William Styron about Sophie, a Holocaust survivor. She had to choose between her two children. One could live, the other had to be killed. – 17 **available** *here:* offered to – 18 **to owe** [əʊ] *schulden* – 26 **livid** very angry – 29 **to dangle** to hang loosely

His uncle sits expressionless before telling me finally, “This is something no one can really understand unless you’ve experienced it yourself.”

Abbreviations

abb	abbreviation (*Abkürzung*)
e.g.	*exempla gratia* (z. B.)
esp	especially
fml	formal
inf	informal
opp	opposite
os	oneself
sb	somebody
sl	slang
sth	something

Bildquellennachweis

Seite 6 Andersen Press, London;
Seite 146 Fotosearch Stock Photography (Digital Wisdom), Waukesha, WI